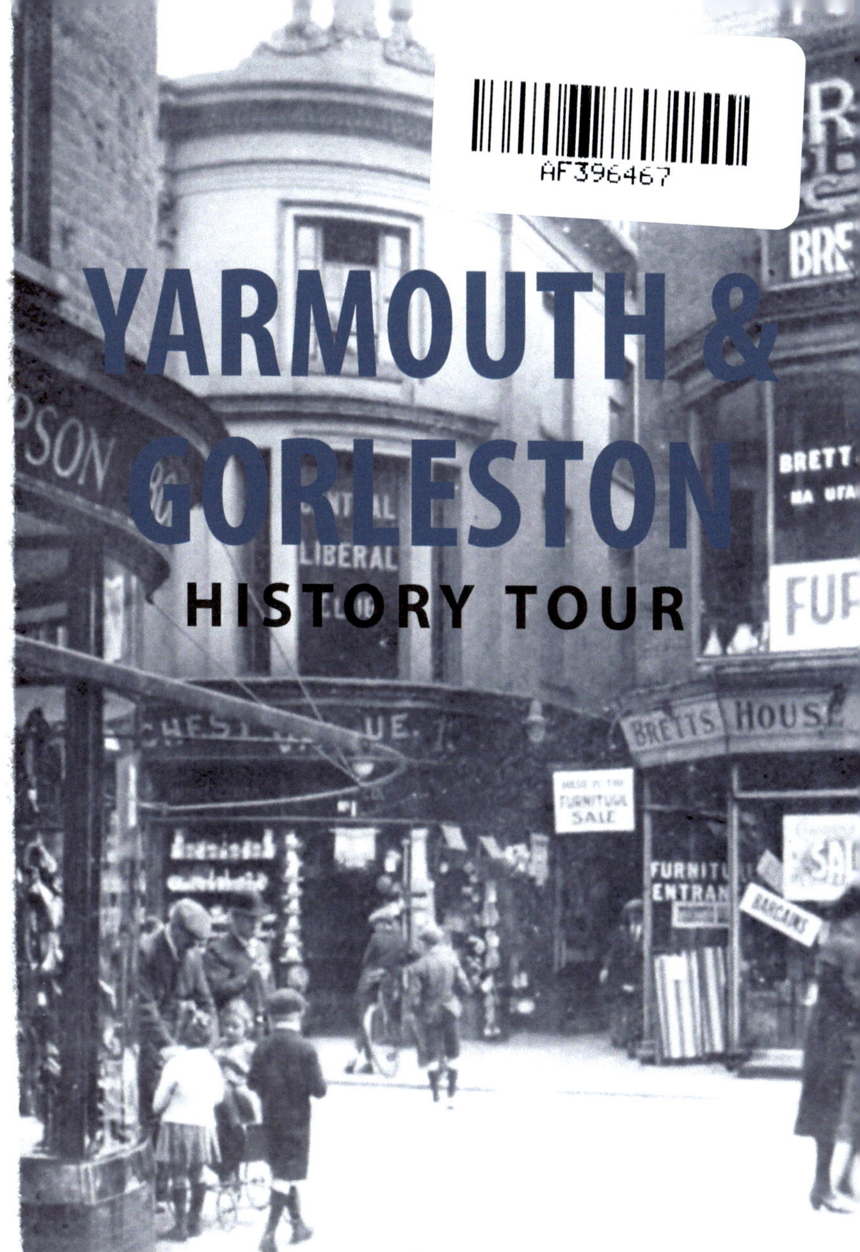

YARMOUTH & GORLESTON

HISTORY TOUR

First published 2009
This edition published 2015

Amberley Publishing
The Hill, Stroud,
Gloucestershire, GL5 4EP
www.amberley-books.com

ISBN 978 1 4456 5446 1 (print)
ISBN 978 1 4456 5447 8 (ebook)

British Library Cataloguing in Publication Data.
A catalogue record for this book is available from the British Library.

Typesetting by Amberley Publishing.
Printed in Great Britain.

Appointed GPSR EU Representative:
Easy Access System Europe Oü,
16879218
Address: Mustamäe tee 50, 10621,
Tallinn, Estonia
Contact Details: gpsr.requests@easproject.com, +358 40 500 3575

INTRODUCTION

Yarmouth rightly insists on calling itself 'Great' and has done so for 800 years. This was originally to distinguish the town from 'Little Yarmouth' across the river Yare: the area that is now called Southtown. The town stands on a sandbank, which only emerged from the sea about 900 years ago. As soon as the sand was dry enough, fishermen settled on it. At first they built rough boathouses and lived in temporary huts, only in use during the fishing season, a form of settlement that was common in those times. Very rapidly, the temporary settlement became permanent, and one sign of this is the establishment of a parish church to cater for the spiritual needs of the fisher folk – and to collect the tithes due to the church: a portion of every boatload of fish caught was claimed by the local rector. A trading market soon followed. This was on the very same site as the present-day market, which is the largest open-air market place in England.

By 1209, the town was important enough to be given its first royal charter, by King John. Yarmouth became one of the most important towns in England in the Middle Ages, as a fishing town and port. Apart from St Nicholas' church, other buildings in Yarmouth from the Middle Ages are also worth going to visit, including the Tolhouse, which is the oldest civic building in Britain, and the town walls with their prominent towers, shown in several images in this book. All the houses in the town were inside the circuit of these walls, a very small area which led to people living in narrow and increasingly crowded alleys running in parallel lines – the famous Rows of Great Yarmouth.

For centuries there was nothing outside the walls, but 250 years ago something happened that changed the character of the town forever – people began to bathe in the sea! This led to the development of the sea front and this process expanded enormously one hundred years later with the coming of the railway. Now people from Norwich could easily visit Yarmouth in a day, and excursion trains were very soon running from London and from the big cities of the Midlands.

Meanwhile, Gorleston, across the Yare, has also flourished. This is on higher ground and there were people living here when Yarmouth was still beneath the sea. It was both a fishing port and a centre for shipbuilding. It became a seaside resort as well, but has always been less boisterous than its neighbour, refusing to develop nearly as many amenities and relying instead on its quieter beauty.

There has been a great change in the last fifty years. The Rows have disappeared and the people who lived in them now live across the river in new houses in Gorleston, Bradwell and Belton. The fishing has gone now, but the wonderful Time and Tide museum tells the fishermen's story. However, the holidaymakers still come to enjoy three miles of golden sands and the activities along the sea front. The town is continuing to develop as a port as well, looking across the North Sea to our neighbours in Europe.

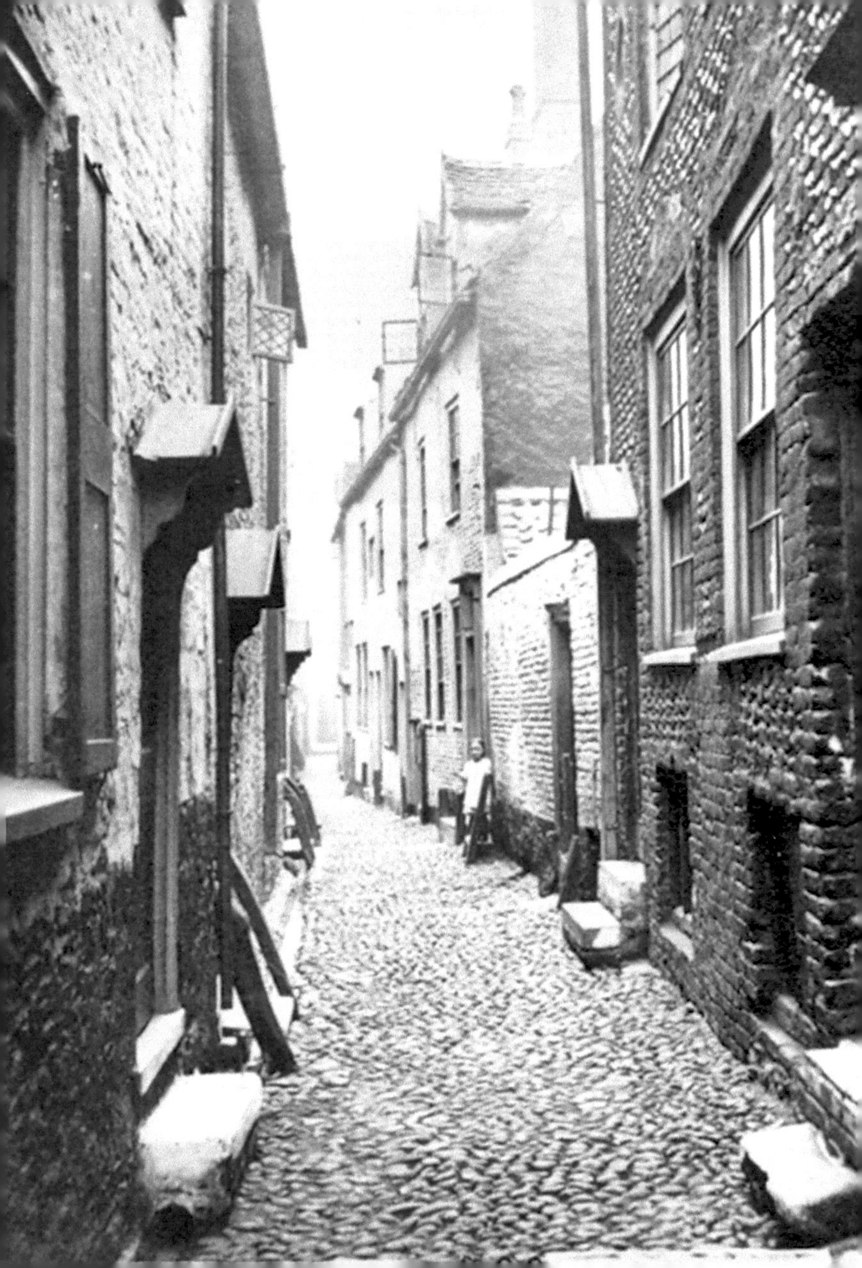

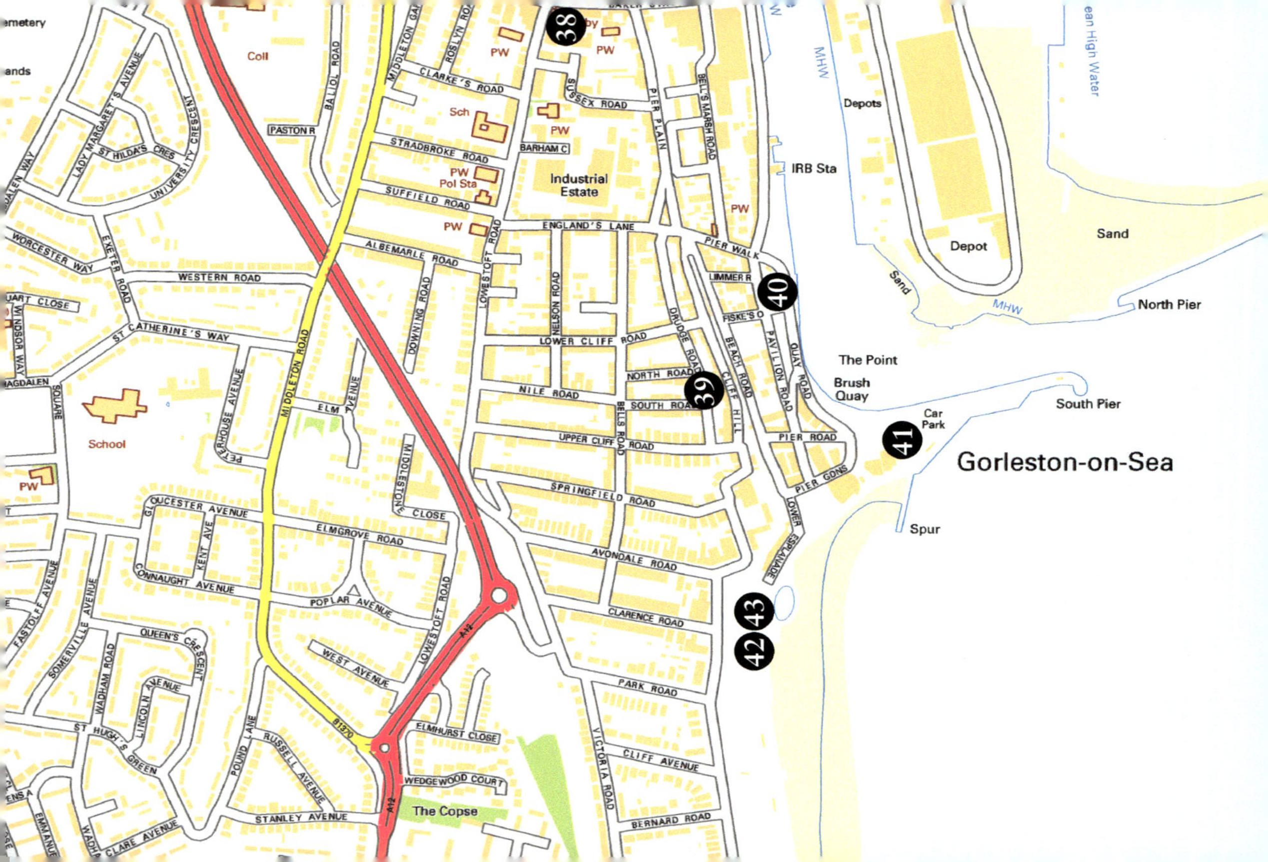

Gorleston-on-Sea
Coll
emetery
ands
Cemetery
MAGDALEN WAY
WINDSOR WAY
STUART CLOSE
MAGDALEN SQUARE
LADY MARGARET'S AVENUE
ST HILDA'S CRES
UNIVERSITY CRESCENT
WORCESTER WAY
EXETER ROAD
ST CATHERINE'S WAY
BALIOL ROAD
PASTON R
MIDDLETON GA
ROSLYN RO
CLARKE'S ROAD
SUSSEX ROAD
BARHAM C
STRADBROKE ROAD
SUFFIELD ROAD
Sch
Pol Sta
PW
PW
PW
PW
PW
Industrial Estate
WESTERN ROAD
ALBEMARLE ROAD
DOWNING ROAD
LOWESTOFT ROAD
ENGLAND'S LANE
NELSON ROAD
LOWER CLIFF ROAD
NILE ROAD
BELLS ROAD
SOUTH ROAD
NORTH ROAD
DRUDGE ROAD
UPPER CLIFF ROAD
SPRINGFIELD ROAD
AVONDALE ROAD
CLARENCE ROAD
PARK ROAD
CLIFF AVENUE
VICTORIA ROAD
BERNARD ROAD
PIER PLAIN
BELL'S MARSH ROAD
PIER WALK
LIMMER R
FISKE'S O
CLIFF HILL
BEACH ROAD
PAVILION ROAD
QUAY ROAD
PIER ROAD
PIER GDNS
LOWER ESPLANADE
The Point
Brush Quay
Car Park
Spur
MHW
MHW
IRB Sta
Depots
Depot
Sand
Sand
North Pier
South Pier
ean High Water
School
PW
ELM AVENUE
PETERHOUSE AVENUE
MIDDLETON ROAD
MIDDLESTON CLOSE
GLOUCESTER AVENUE
KENT AVE
ELMGROVE ROAD
CONNAUGHT AVENUE
POPLAR AVENUE
LOWESTOFT ROAD
WEST AVENUE
ELMHURST CLOSE
WEDGEWOOD COURT
The Copse
FASTOLFF AVENUE
SOMERVILLE AVENUE
WADHAM ROAD
QUEEN'S CRESCENT
ST HUGH'S GREEN
LINCOLN AVENUE
POUND LANE
RUSSELL AVENUE
STANLEY AVENUE
CLARE AVENUE
EMMANUEL
A12
A12
B1370
38
39
40
41
42
43

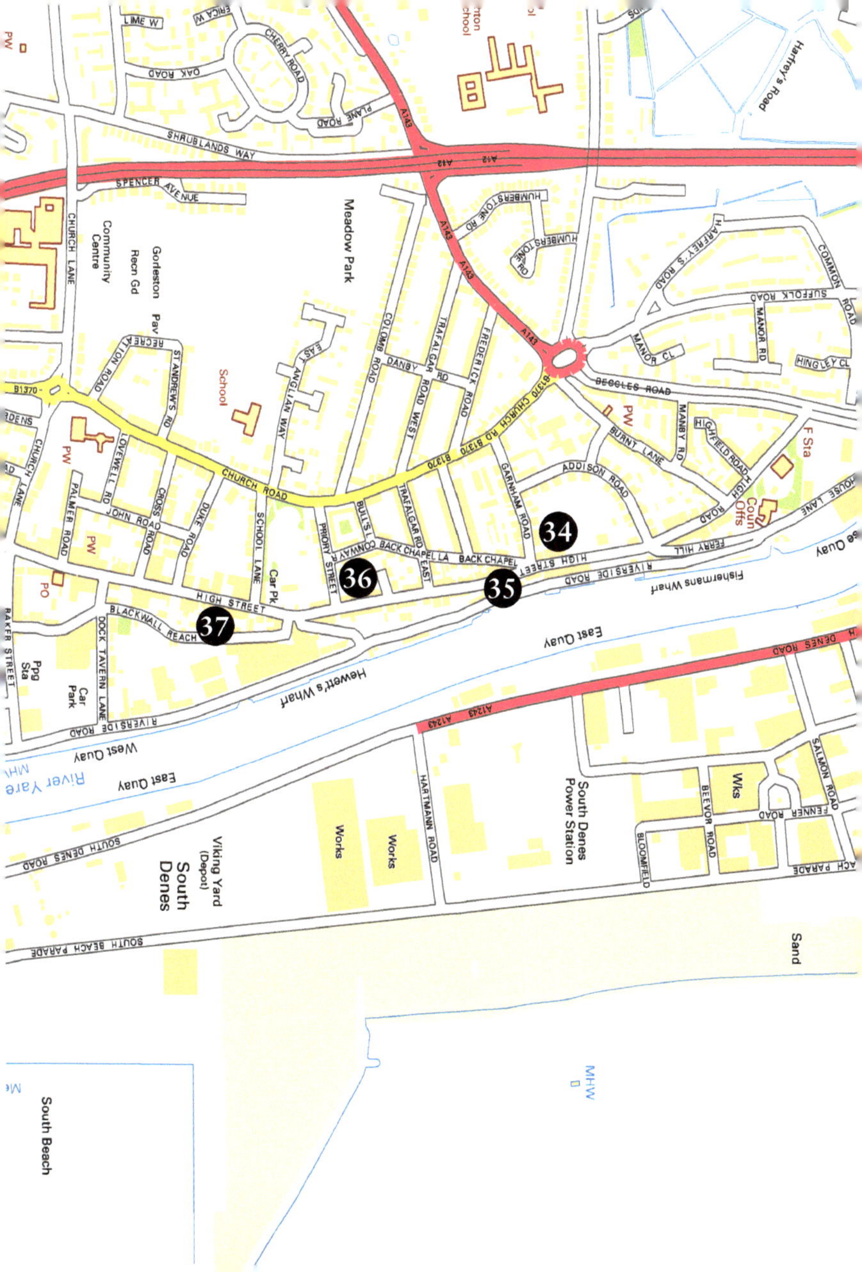

LIME W
CHERRY ROAD
OAK ROAD
PLANE ROAD
SHRUBLANDS WAY
SPENCER AVENUE
Meadow Park
HUMBERSTONE RD
HUMBERSTONE RD
HARFREY'S ROAD
A12
A12
A143
A143
CHURCH LANE
Community Centre
Gorleston Recn Gd
Pav
RECREATION ROAD
ST ANDREW'S RD
School
EAST ANGLIAN WAY
COLOMB ROAD
DANBY ROAD
TRAFALGAR RD
FREDERICK ROAD
A143
CHURCH RD B1370
HARFREY'S ROAD
COMMON ROAD
SUFFOLK ROAD
MANOR RD
HINGLEY CL
MANOR CL
B1370
BECCLES ROAD
MANBY RD
PW
BURNT LANE
HIGHFIELD ROAD
HIGH ROAD
F Sta
Coun Offs
B1370
CHURCH ROAD
TRAFALGAR RD WEST
GARNHAM ROAD
ADDISON ROAD
HOUSE LANE
FERRY HILL
B1370
CHURCH RD
School Lane
Car Pk
PRIORY STREET
BULL'S L
CONWAY
BACK CHAPEL LA
BACK CHAPEL EAST
BACK CHAPEL
HIGH STREET
RIVERSIDE ROAD
Fishermans Wharf
se Quay
PW
PALMER ROAD
LOVEWELL RD
JOHN ROAD
CROSS ROAD
DUKE ROAD
PW
PO
HIGH STREET
BLACKWALL REACH
RAKER STREET
DOCK TAVERN LANE
Ppg Sta
Car Park
RIVERSIDE ROAD
Hewett's Wharf
East Quay
DENES ROAD
A1243
CHURCH LANE
B1370
DENS
34
35
36
37
West Quay
East Quay
River Yare
MHW
SOUTH DENES ROAD
South Denes
Viking Yard (Depot)
HARTMANN ROAD
Works
Works
South Denes Power Station
A1243 A1243
SALMON ROAD
FENNER ROAD
Wks
BEEVOR ROAD
BLOOMFIELD
ACH PARADE
MHW
Sand
SOUTH BEACH PARADE
South Beach
Me
PW
PW

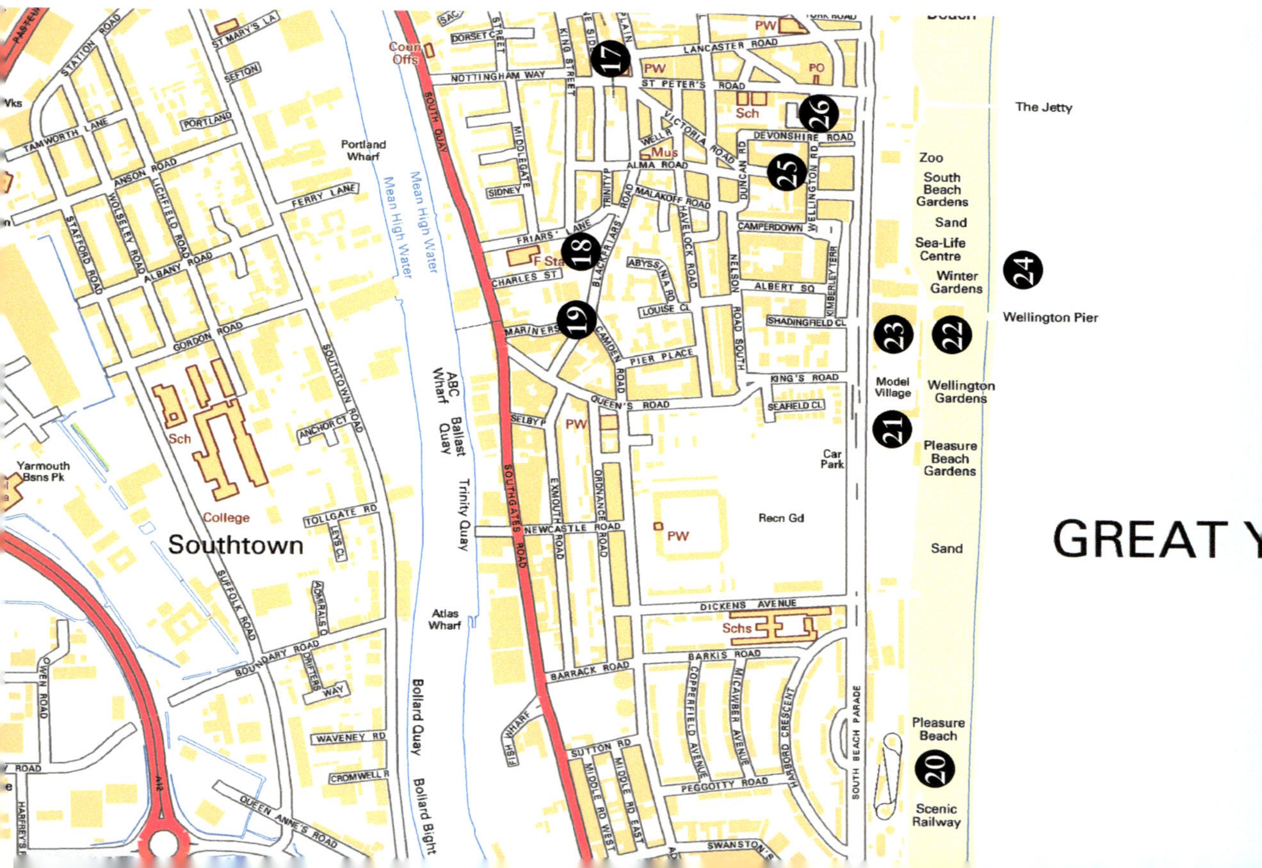

Southtown
College
Sch
GREAT Y
HARFREY'S ROAD
OWEN ROAD
QUEEN ANNE'S ROAD
CROMWELL R
WAVENEY RD
DRIFTERS WAY
ADMIRALS Q
BOUNDARY ROAD
SUFFOLK ROAD
TOLGATE RD
LEYS CL
ANCHOR CT
SOUTHTOWN ROAD
GORDON ROAD
ALBANY ROAD
STAFFORD ROAD
WOLSELEY ROAD
LICHFIELD ROAD
ANSON ROAD
TAMWORTH LANE
STATION ROAD
PASTEUR
PORTLAND
SEFTON
ST MARY'S LA
FERRY LANE
Portland Wharf
Yarmouth Bsns Pk
A12
Bollard Bight
Bollard Quay
Atlas Wharf
Trinity Quay
Ballast Quay
ABC Wharf
Mean High Water
Mean High Water
SOUTH QUAY
Count Offs
FISH WHARF
SUTTON RD
MIDDLE RD WEST
MIDDLE RD EAST
BARRACK ROAD
NEWCASTLE ROAD
EXMOUTH ROAD
ORDNANCE ROAD
SOUTHGATES ROAD
SELBY P
QUEEN'S ROAD
CAMDEN ROAD
MARINERS
CHARLES ST
FRIARS LANE
F Sta
BLACKFRIARS ROAD
SIDNEY
MIDDLEGATE
NOTTINGHAM WAY
DORSET CL
ST STREET
KING STREET
SAC
PW
Copperfield Avenue
PEGGOTTY ROAD
MICAWBER AVENUE
SWANSTON'S
BARKIS ROAD
DICKENS AVENUE
Schs
HARBORD CRESCENT
SOUTH BEACH PARADE
Recn Gd
PW
PIER PLACE
LOUISE CL
ABYSSINIA RD
HAVELOCK ROAD
NELSON ROAD SOUTH
SEAFIELD CL
KING'S ROAD
SHADINGFIELD CL
ALBERT SQ
KIMBERLEY TERR
CAMPERDOWN
DUNCAN RD
WELLINGTON RD
MALAKOFF ROAD
ALMA ROAD
VICTORIA ROAD
Mus
TRINITY P
PLAIN
WELL
DEVONSHIRE ROAD
Sch
PO
ST PETER'S ROAD
LANCASTER ROAD
PW
Car Park
Model Village
Wellington Gardens
Wellington Pier
Pleasure Beach Gardens
Sand
Winter Gardens
Sea-Life Centre
South Beach Gardens
Sand
Zoo
Scenic Railway
Pleasure Beach
The Jetty
17
18
19
20
21
22
23
24
25
26

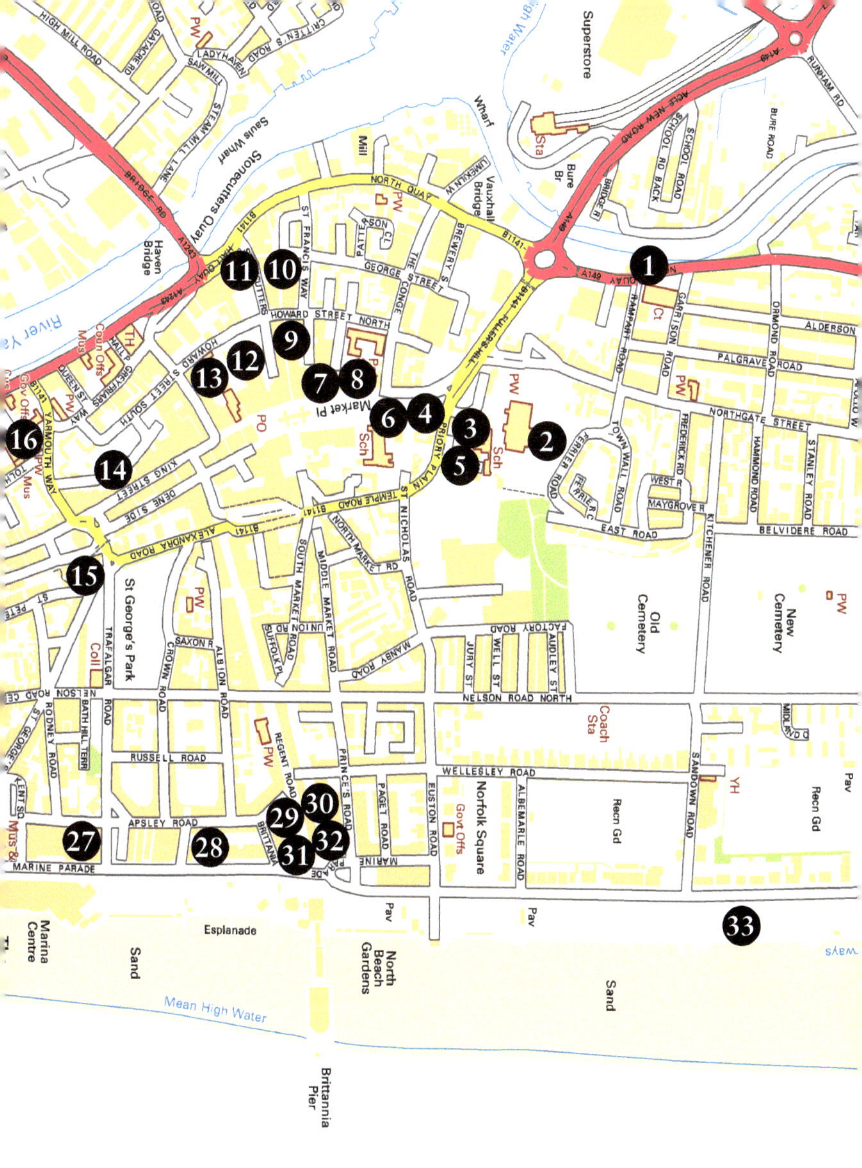

Superstore
Wharf
Mill
HIGH MILL ROAD
GARAGE RD
SAW MILL
LADYHAVEN
CRITTEN'S ROAD
STEAM MILL LANE
Sauls Wharf
Stonecutters Quay
Haven Bridge
River Yare
Coun Offs
TH
Govt Offs Mus
YARMOUTH WAY
QUEEN ST
GREYFRIARS WAY
NORTH QUAY
THE CONGE
GEORGE STREET
BREWERY S
PATTERSON CL
Vauxhall Bridge
LIMEKILN WK
Sta
Bure Br
SCHOOL ROAD
SCHOOL RD BACK
BRIDGE R
BURE ROAD
RUNHAM RD
RAMPART ROAD
GARRISON
ORMOND ROAD
ALDERSON
PALGRAVE ROAD
NORTHGATE STREET
FERRIER ROAD
TOWN WALL ROAD
FREDERICK RD
HAMMOND ROAD
STANLEY ROAD
MAYGROVE R
WEST R
EAST ROAD
BELVIDERE ROAD
KITCHENER ROAD
Old Cemetery
New Cemetery
PW
ST FRANCIS WAY
HOWARD STREET NORTH
HOWARD STREET SOUTH
KING STREET
DENE SIDE
Market Pl
PO
Sch
PRIORY PLAIN
ST NICHOLAS ROAD
TEMPLE ROAD
ALEXANDRA ROAD
SOUTH MARKET ROAD
MIDDLE MARKET ROAD
NORTH MARKET RD
MANBY ROAD
UNION RD
SUFFOLK PL
SAXON R
ALBION ROAD
CROWN ROAD
NELSON ROAD NORTH
JURY ST
WELL ST
AUDLEY ST
FACTORY ROAD
St George's Park
Coll
TRAFALGAR ROAD
BATH HILL TERR
NELSON ROAD CE
RODNEY ROAD
ST GEORGE'S
KENT SQ
Mus &
RUSSELL ROAD
APSLEY ROAD
REGENT ROAD
BRITANNIA
PRINCE'S ROAD
PAGET ROAD
MARINE PARADE
EUSTON ROAD
WELLESLEY ROAD
Norfolk Square
ALBEMARLE ROAD
Govt Offs
Coach Sta
SANDOWN ROAD
MIDLAND ROAD
YH
Recn Gd
Pav
MARINE PARADE
Marina Centre
Sand
Esplanade
North Beach Gardens
Sand
Pav
Mean High Water
Brittania Pier
ways

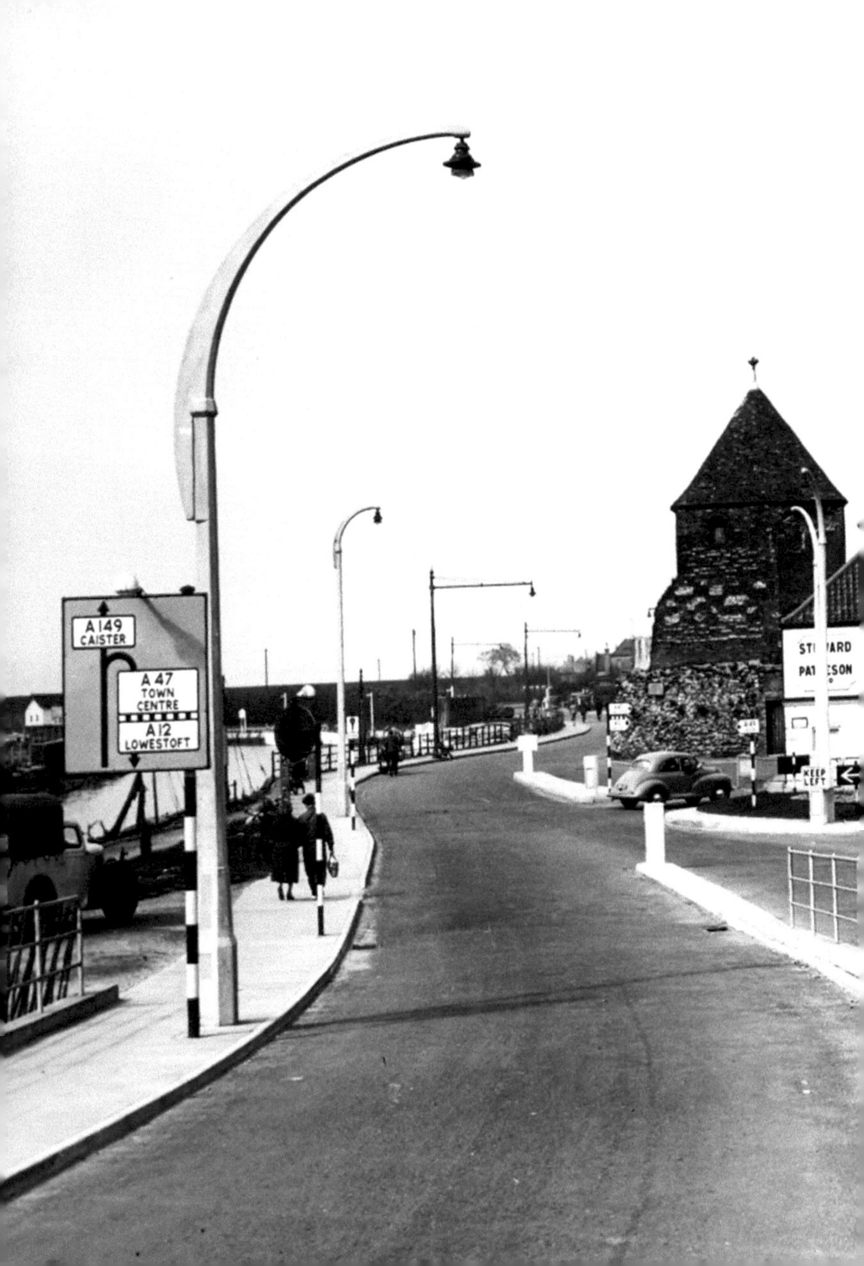

A149
CAISTER
A 47
TOWN
CENTRE
A12
LOWESTOFT
STEWARD
PATTESON
KEEP
LEFT

1. THE NORTH-WEST TOWER AND THE SWAN

The North-West Tower is the northern limit of the medieval town wall, which ran east behind the Swan and on the line of the terraced houses to the right, to the churchyard and the North-East Tower. The wall then ran to the south to the towers shown in other pictures in this book. It then turned sharp right and ran due west to the river.

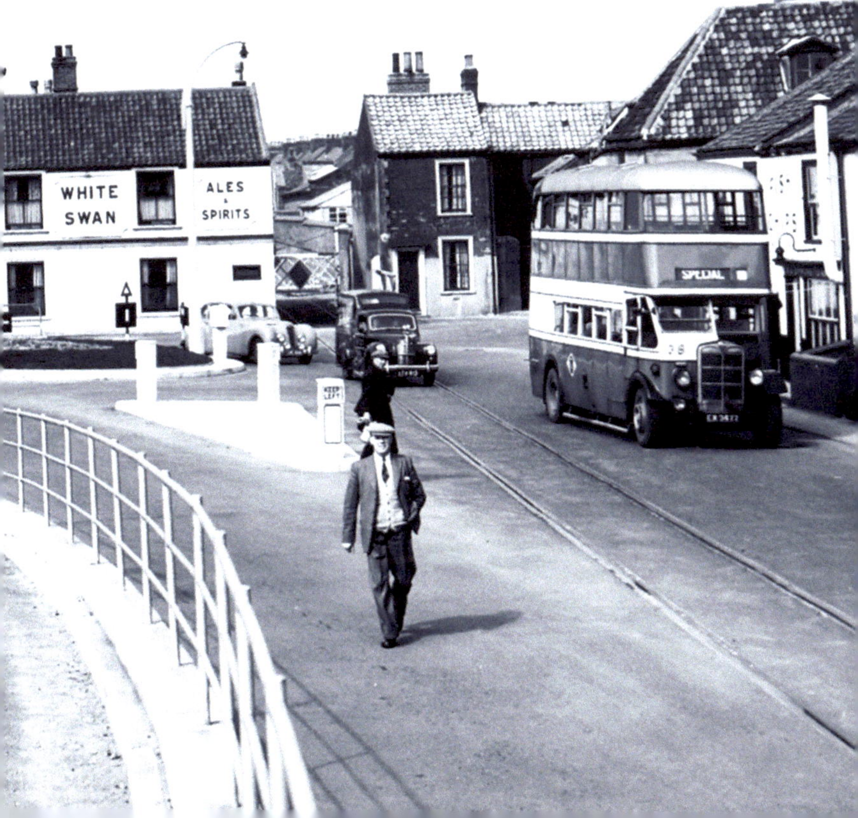

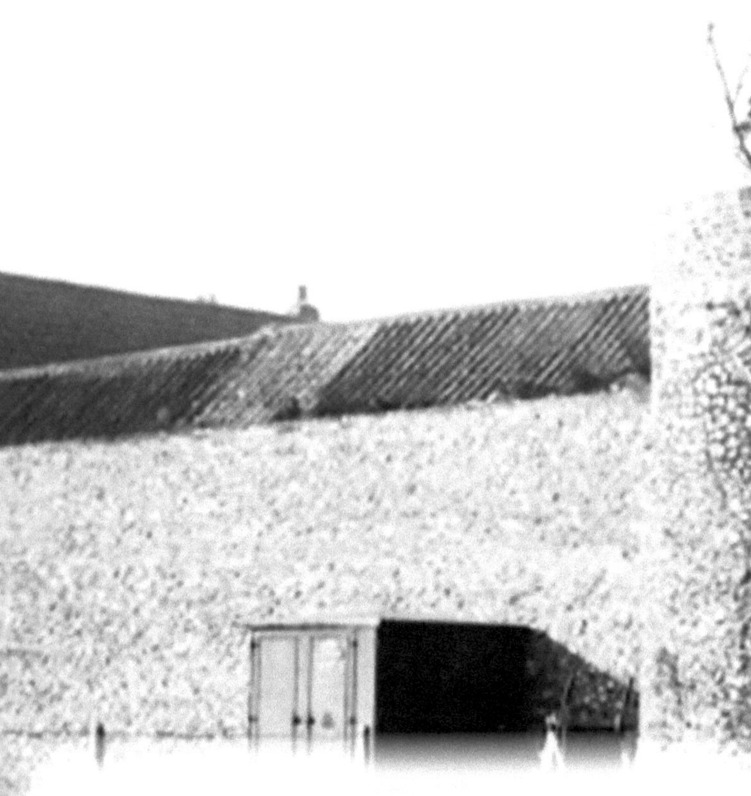

2. THE NORTH-EAST TOWER

Only five minutes' walk from the busy Market Place, this is one of the parts of central Yarmouth where the town walls can be seen most clearly; we are standing outside the medieval town, facing what the Tudor poet Thomas Nash called 'a flinty ring of sixteen towers ready to send out thunder to any Spaniard who dared to come near'. Today, Spanish visitors are most welcome in Yarmouth, along with visitors from every country!

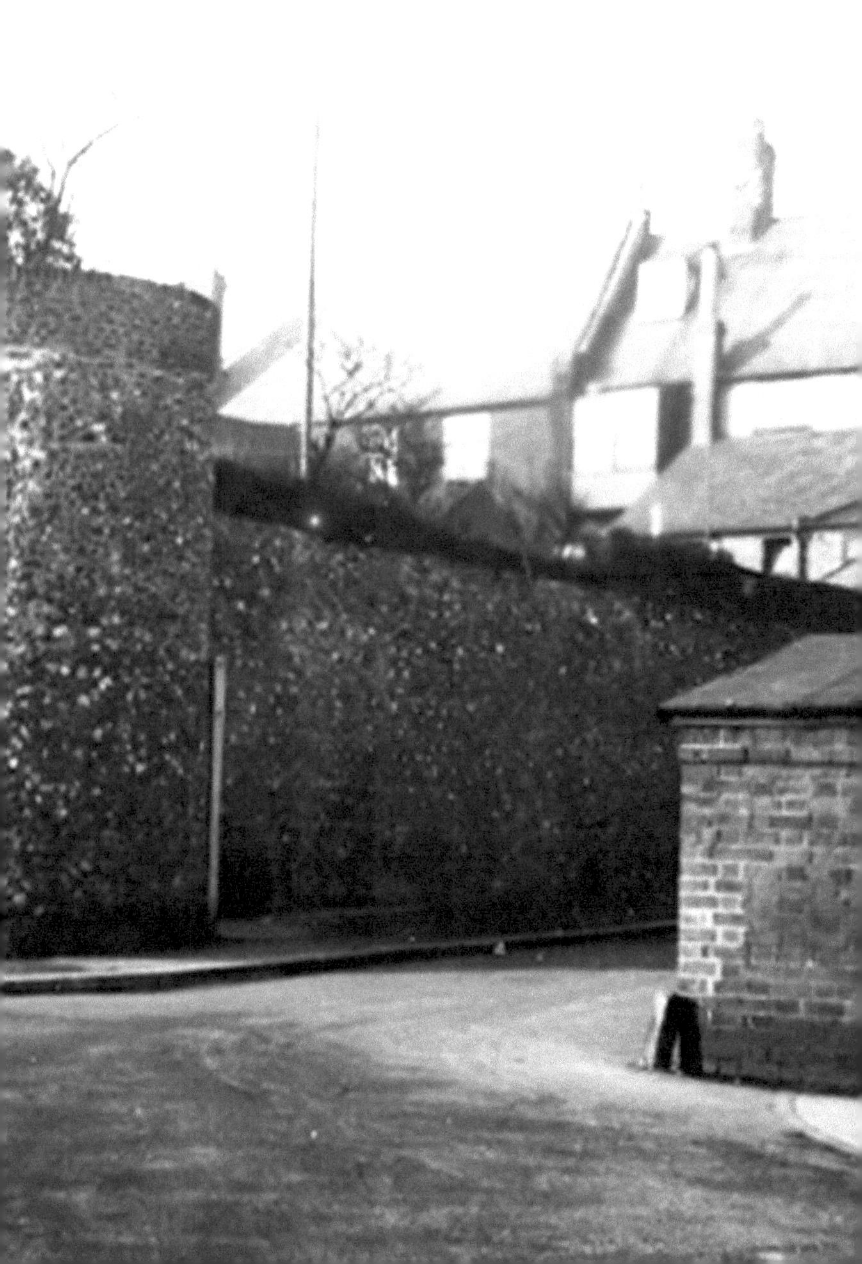

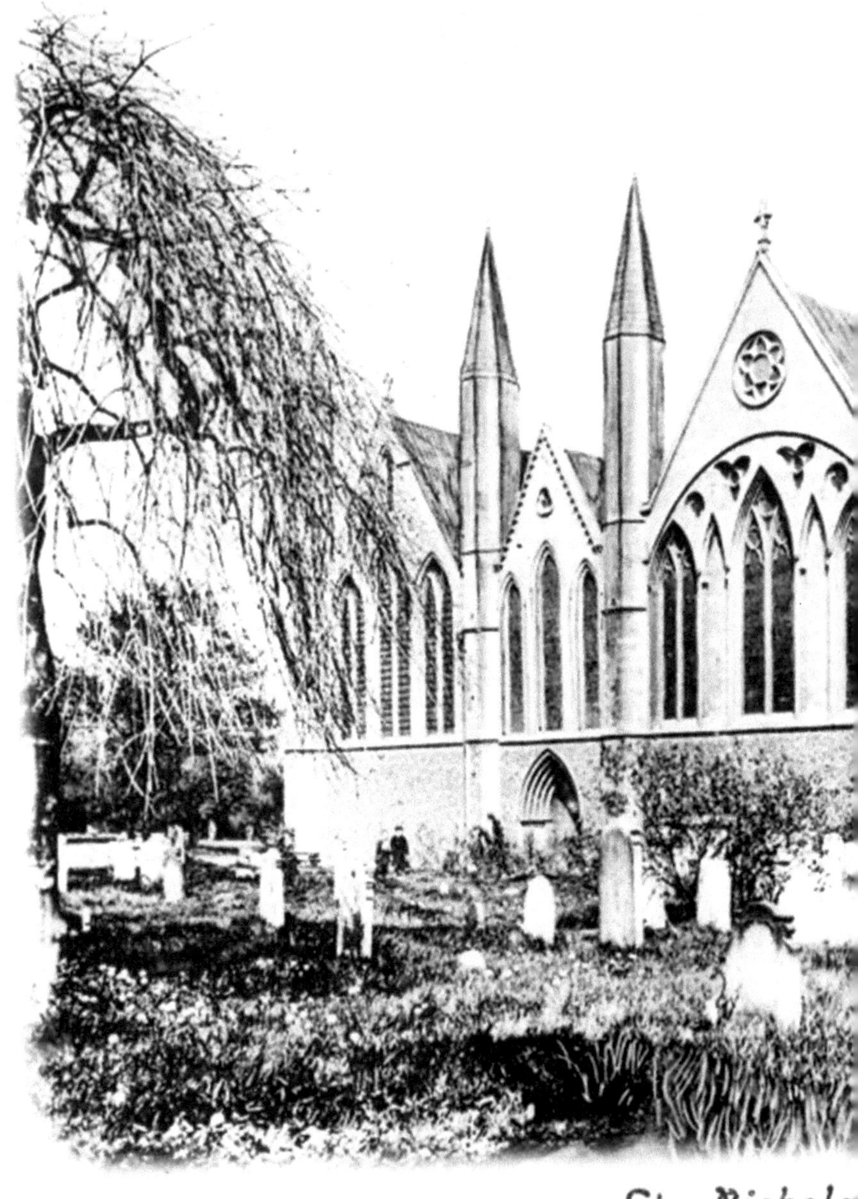

St. Nichola[s]

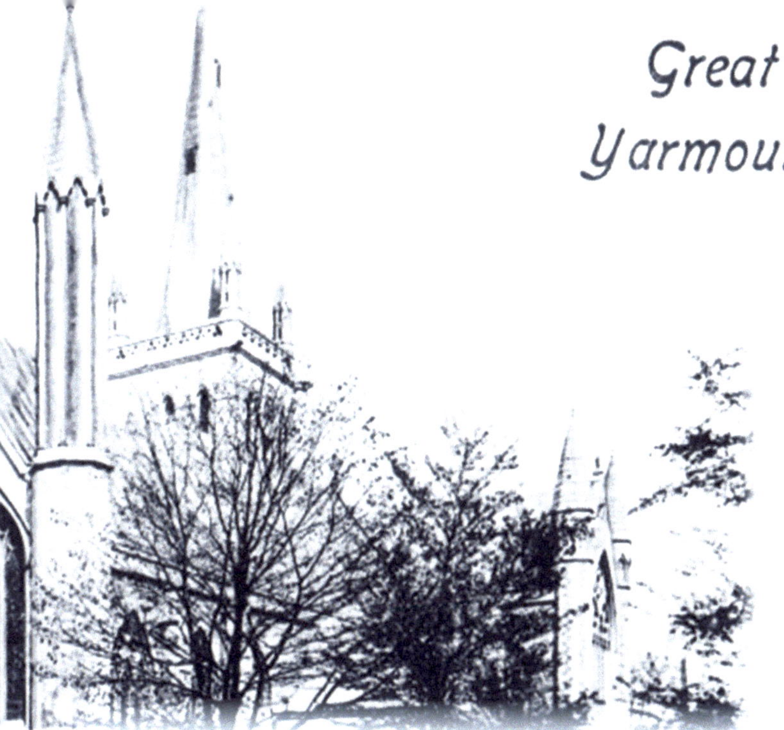

3. ST NICHOLAS' CHURCH FROM THE MARKET PLACE

The church is sometimes said to be the largest parish church in England. In 1757, John Price saw some verses in the window of the Wrestlers that began:

The Yarmouth girls are one and all. Straight as their steeple though not quite as tall.

The point of the poem is that the spire at that time was not straight but twisted! That spire was replaced in the early nineteenth century with a shorter spire, which was itself destroyed by bombs in 1942.

4. CHURCH PLAIN

The photograph here shows a public meeting in Church Plain in 1907. The churchyard is behind the trees on the left, surrounded by a high fence which was put in almost two centuries ago and was to deter people from stealing bodies from the churchyard to sell to anatomists in London. One of the rows near here even became known as 'Body-Snatchers Row'.

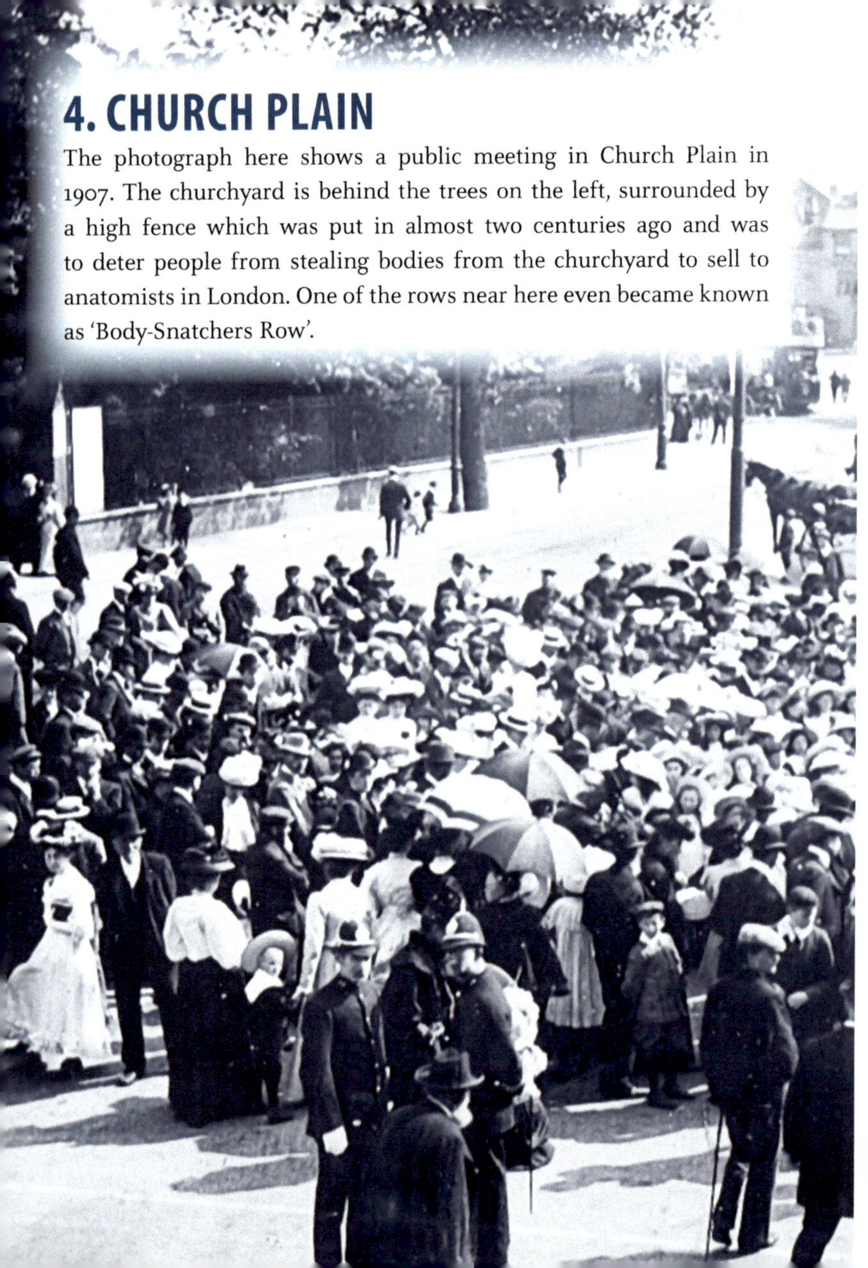

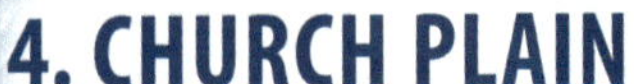

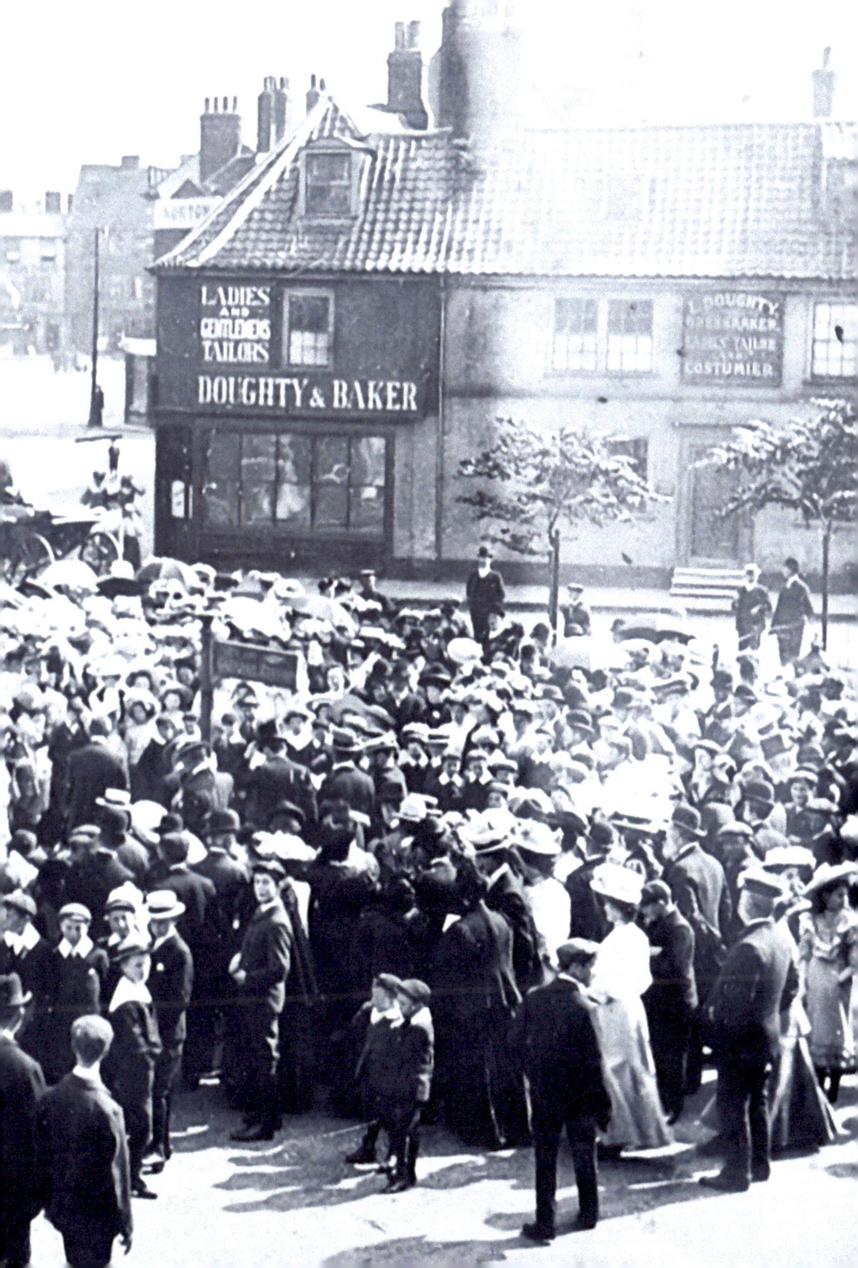

LADIES AND GENTLEMENS TAILORS
DOUGHTY & BAKER
L. DOUGHTY
DRESSMAKER
LADIES TAILOR AND
COSTUMIER

5. THE PRIORY SCHOOL

The hall of the medieval priory was reused as a charity school for poor children in the 1840s. The church of Saint Nicholas can be seen behind; the original priory was for monks who served the church. The school buildings were once said to be haunted by the ghost of an Egyptian mummy, a story told in full in my book, *Paranormal Norfolk*!

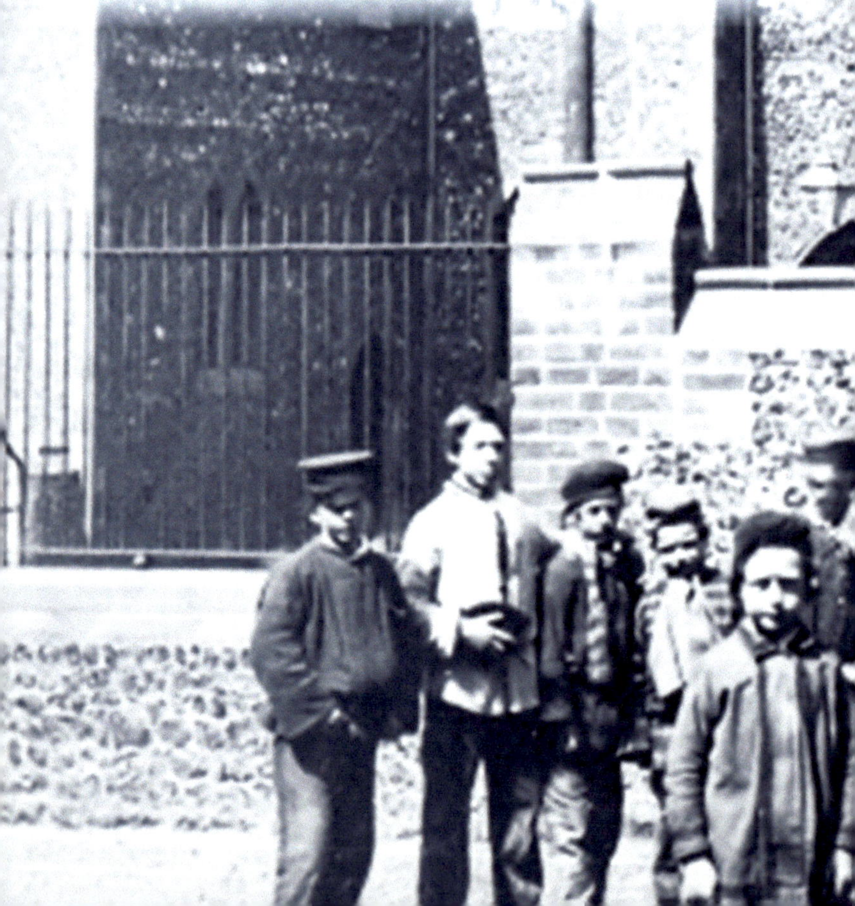

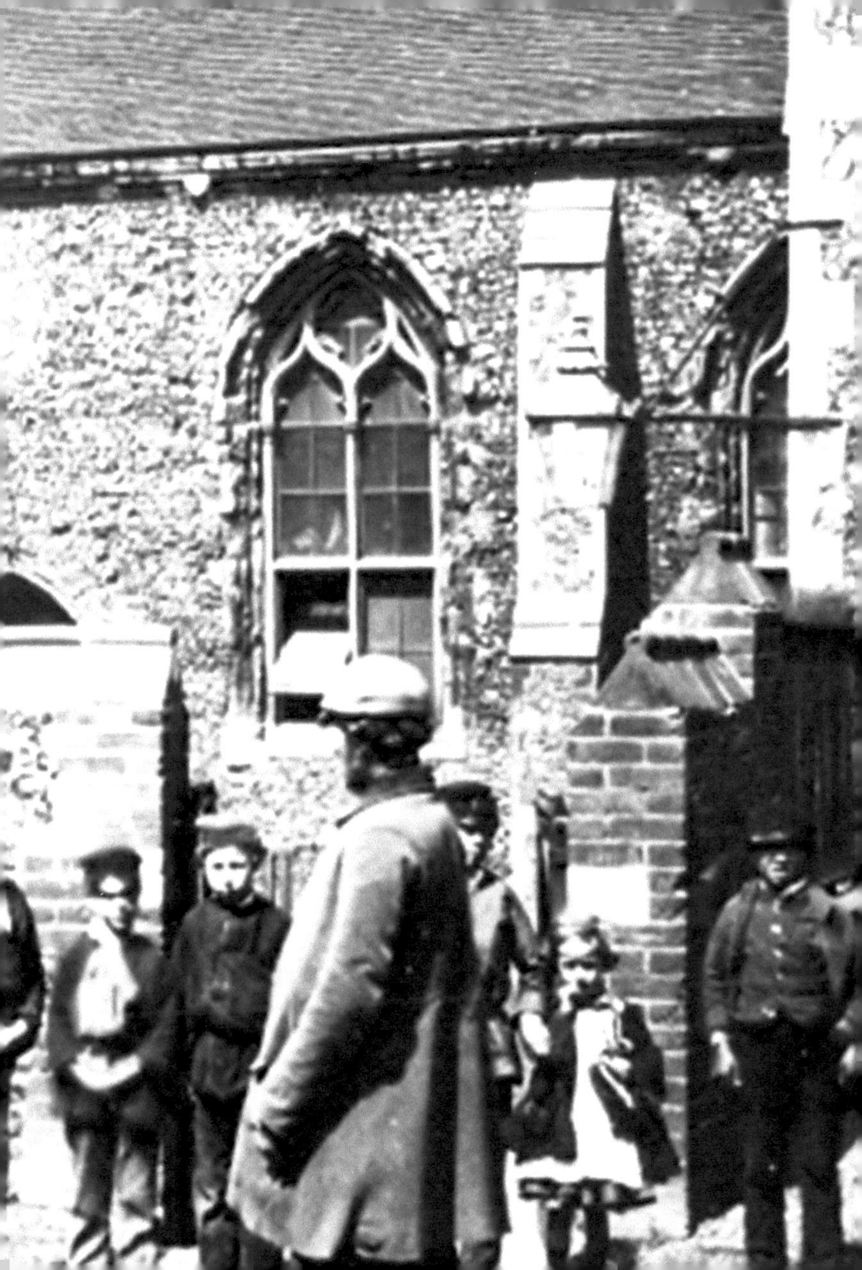

6. THE FISHERMEN'S HOSPITAL

The Fishermen's Hospital was built for 'decayed fishermen' in 1702. The statue in the yard is of 'charity', and there is a plaster relief of a sailing ship in the pediment – which as Nikolaus Pevsner noted, 'is clearly proceeding backwards'! The Dutch-style gables give a Continental atmosphere to this end of Yarmouth Market place.

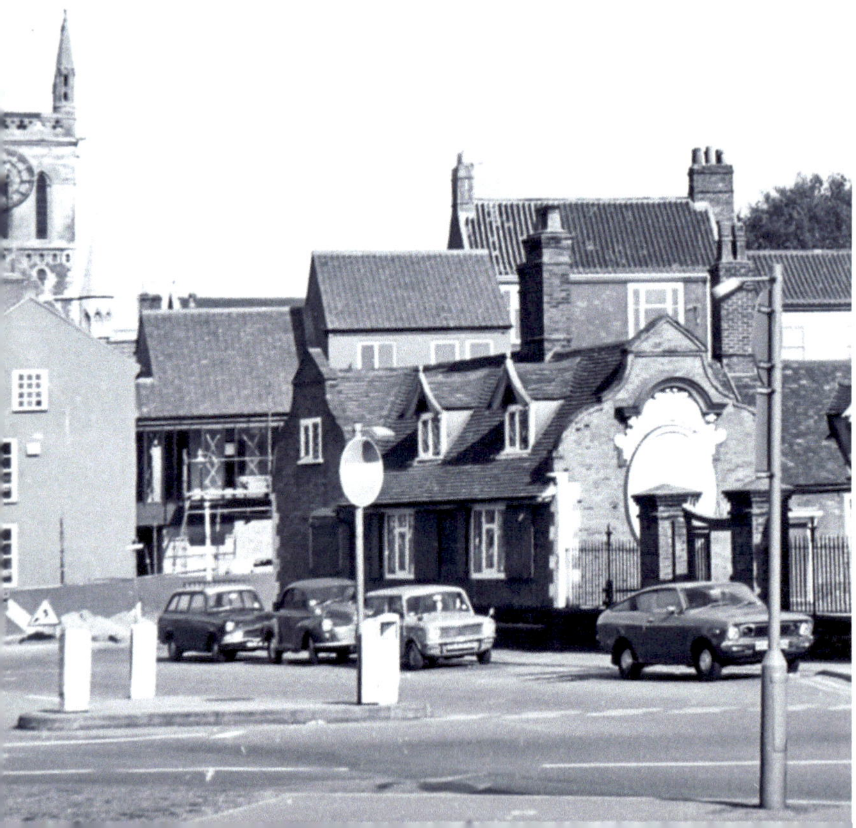

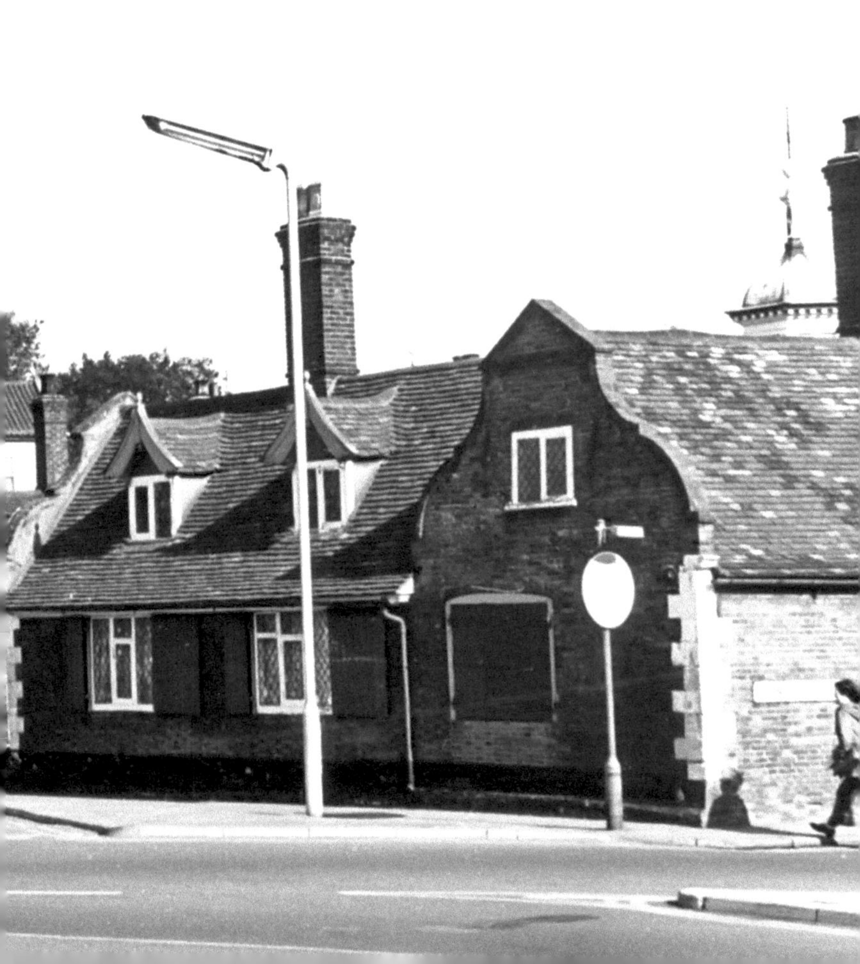

7. CHURCH AND MARKET

The Church and the Market Place together make up the heart of the ancient town, the first part to develop as the sandbank on which Yarmouth now stands slowly emerged from the sea. The ground falls (slightly) away in all direction from this 'high' point. The market is the largest open-air market in England.

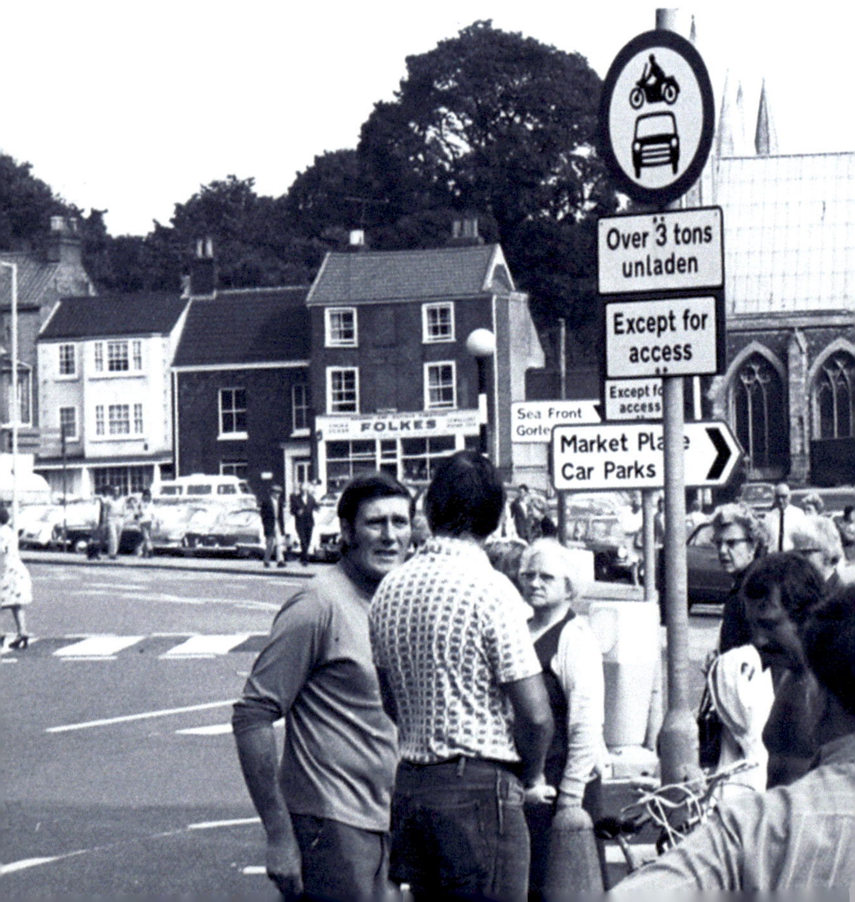

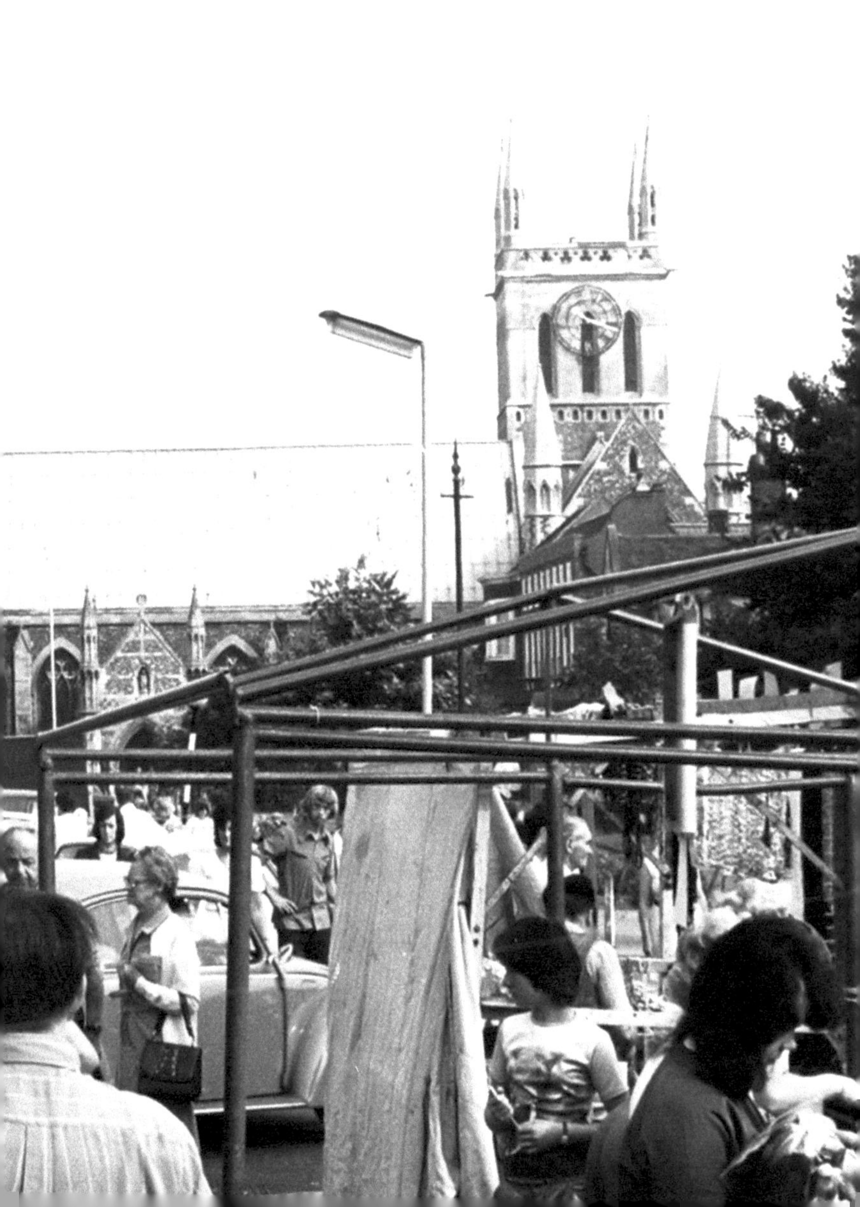

8. THE MARKET PLACE

A 1906 guide book says of the market:

> On its stalls are exposed in tempting array the rich produce of the fertile counties of Norfolk and Suffolk, brought hither by buxom farm-wives and cream-complexioned cottagers, whose appearance is as good a testimony to the health-giving purity of the East Anglian air as the quality of the poultry, fruit and vegetables is to the richness of the soil.

Has the market changed over the last century?

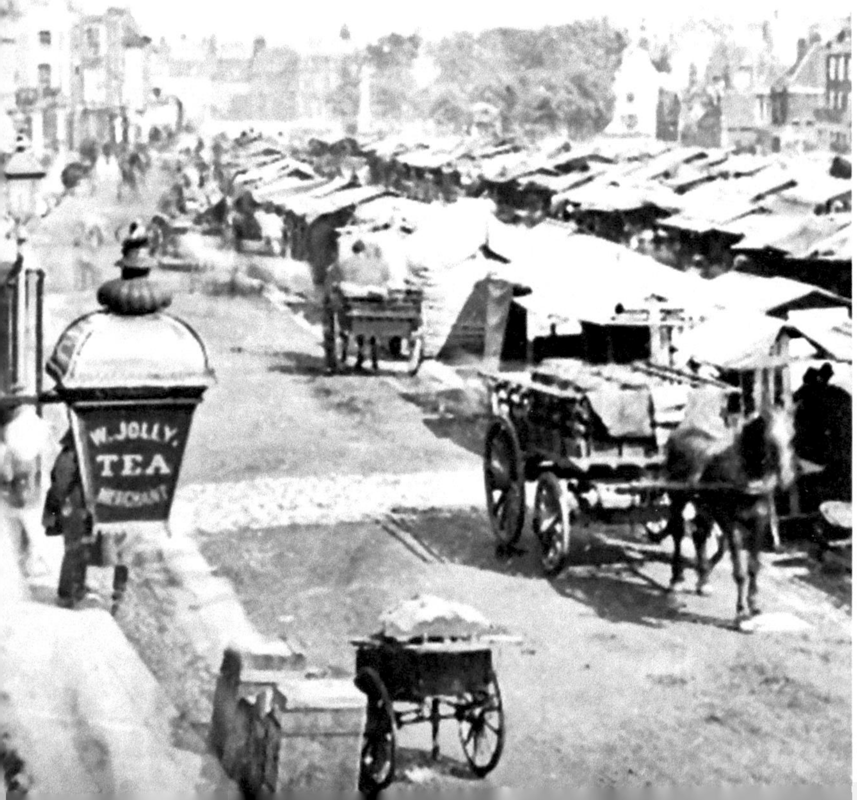

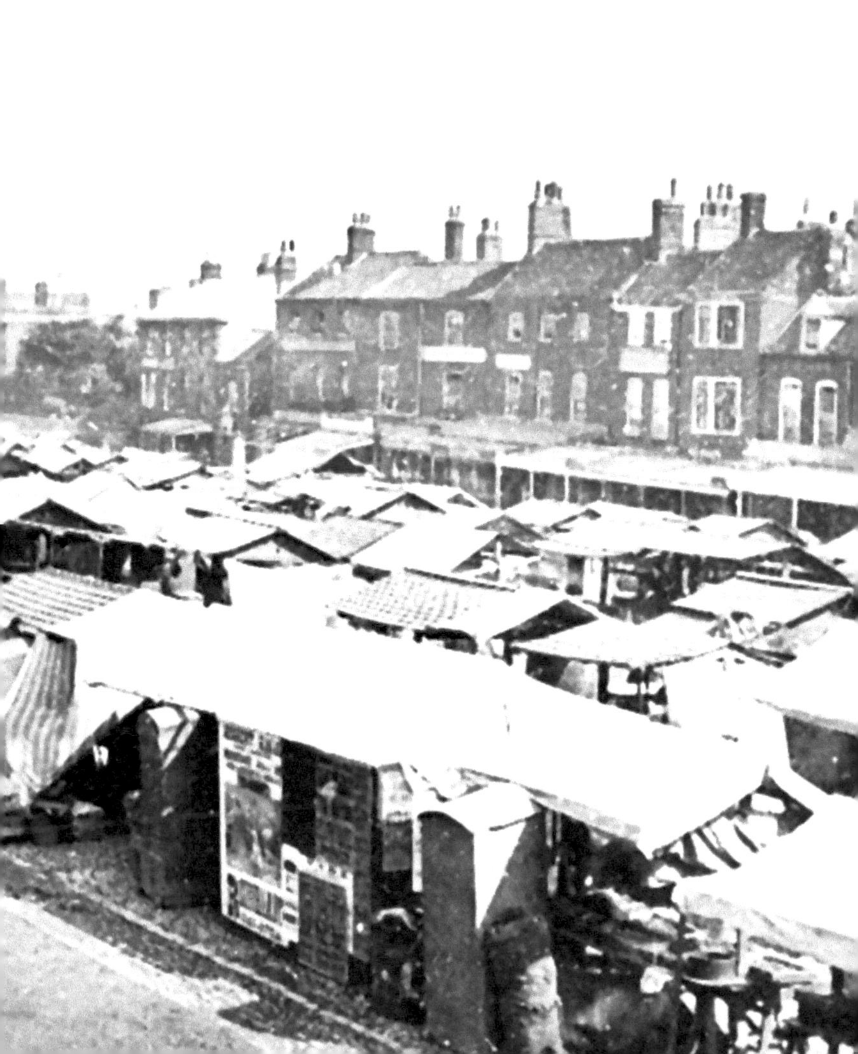

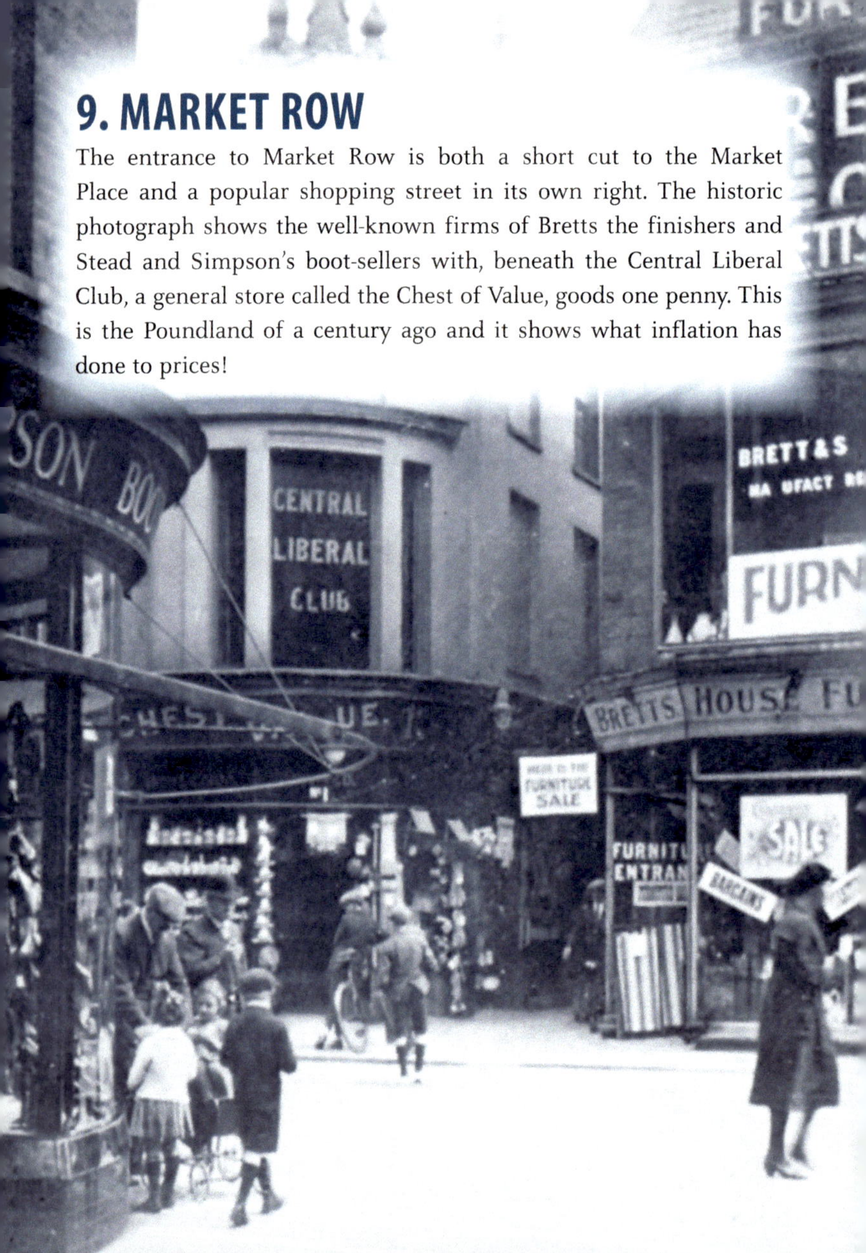

9. MARKET ROW

The entrance to Market Row is both a short cut to the Market Place and a popular shopping street in its own right. The historic photograph shows the well-known firms of Bretts the finishers and Stead and Simpson's boot-sellers with, beneath the Central Liberal Club, a general store called the Chest of Value, goods one penny. This is the Poundland of a century ago and it shows what inflation has done to prices!

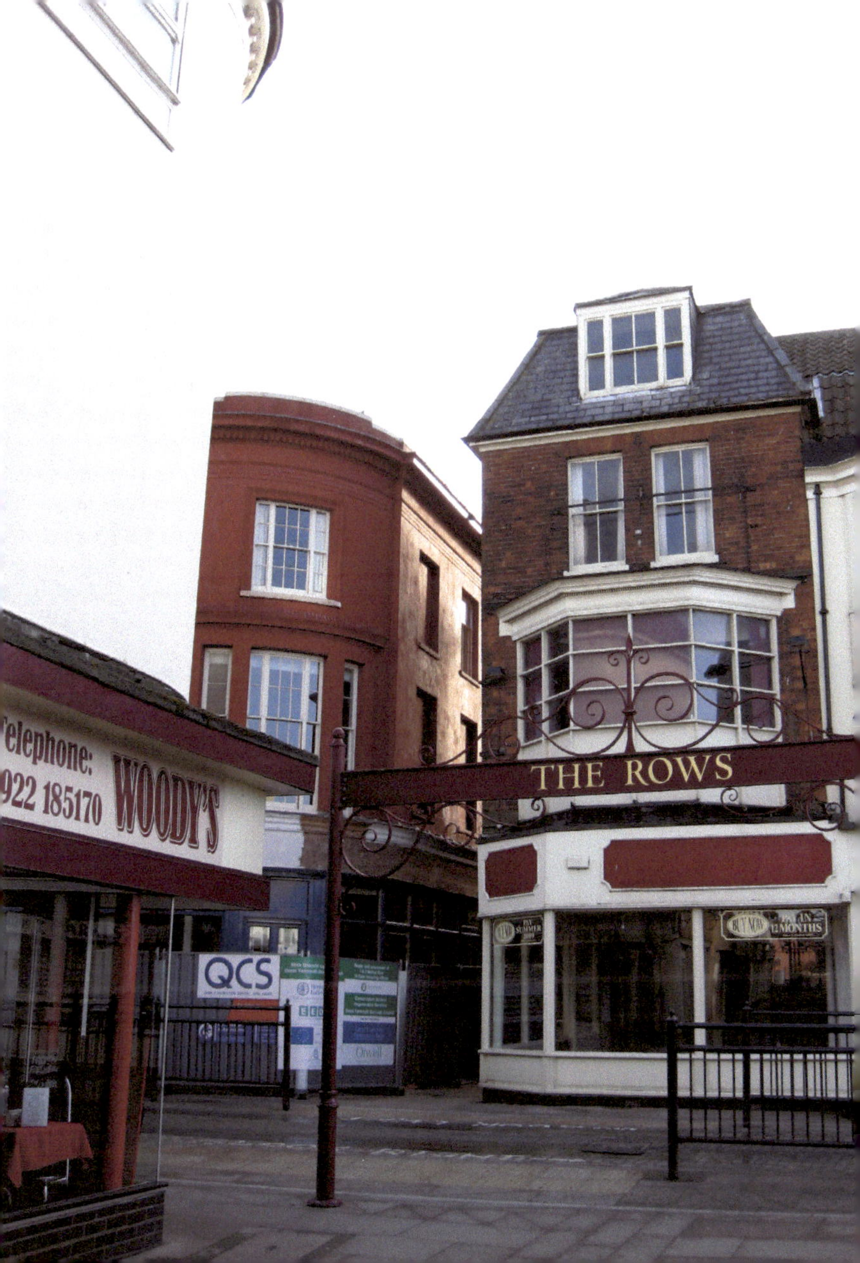
Telephone:
922 185170
WOODY'S
QCS
THE ROWS
PAY SUMMER
BUY NOW
IN 12 MONTHS
Orwell

10. INSIDE BROAD ROW

Broad and Market Rows are the only two of the 145 rows to survive in a complete state and they are not typical: most of the other rows were much narrower, and were made up of houses rather than shops. Traders in the Row included Lambert's, the tea dealers.

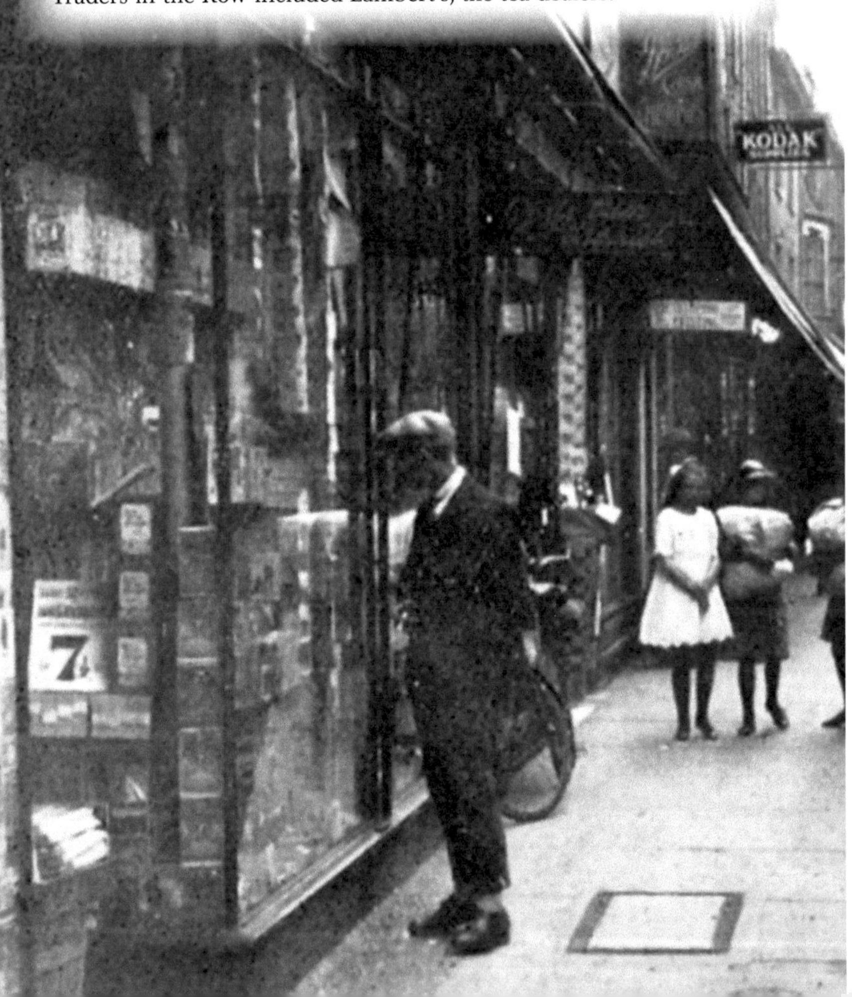

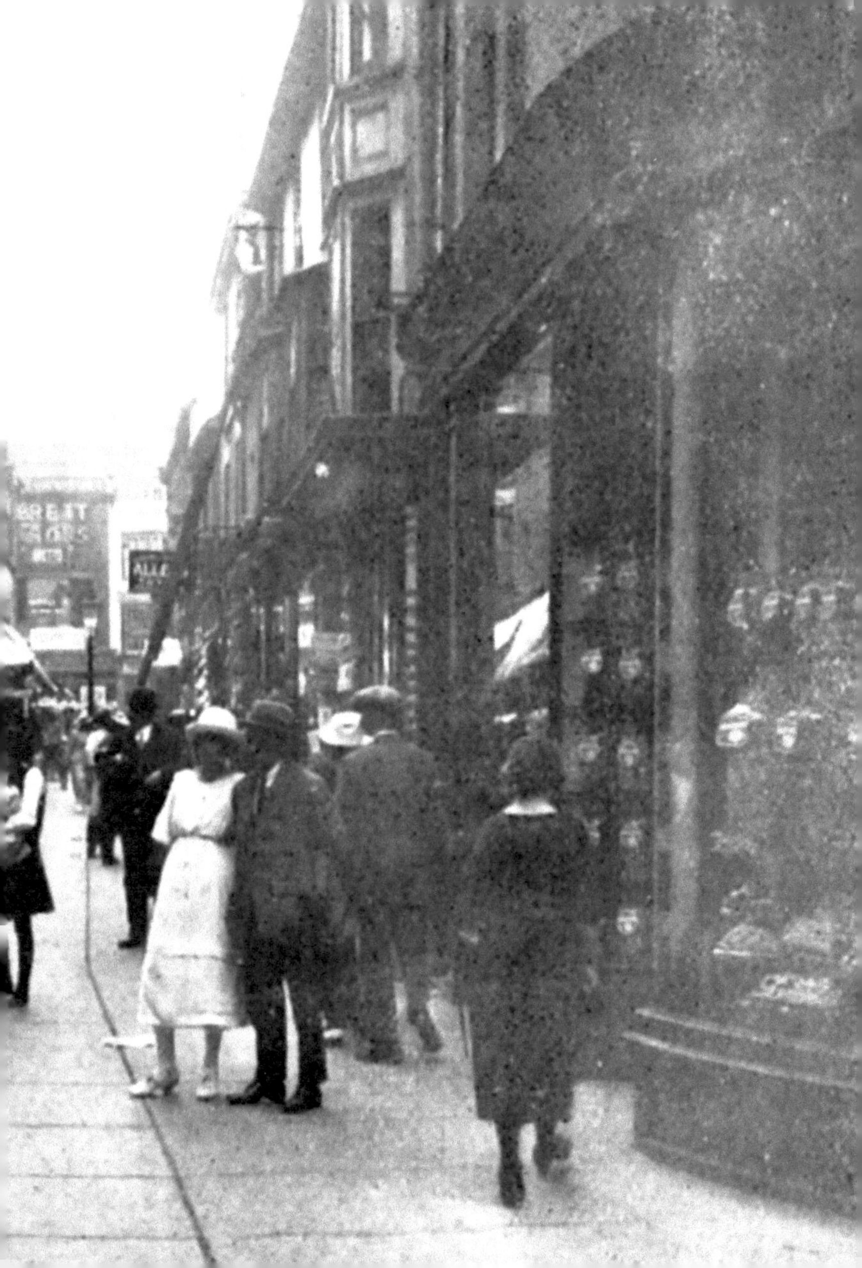

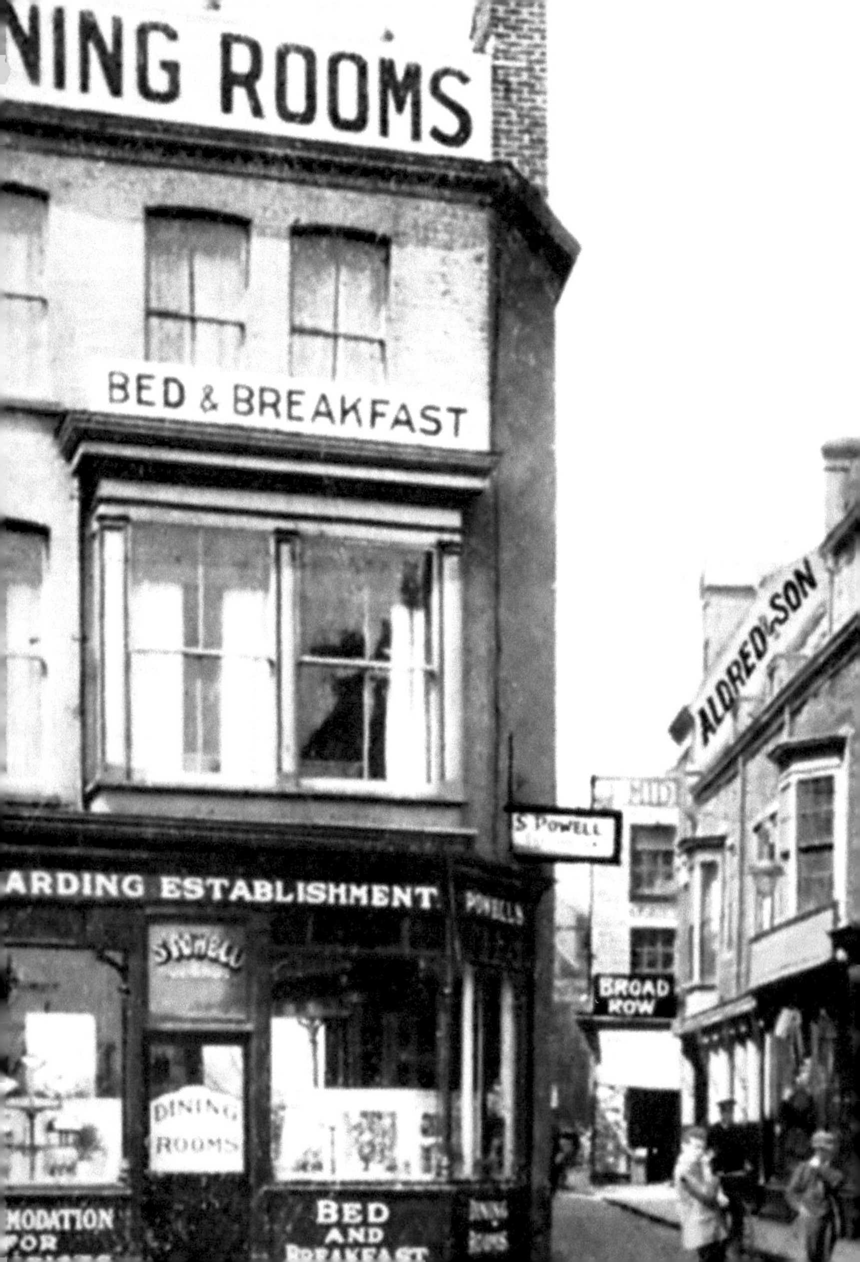
NING ROOMS
BED & BREAKFAST
ARDING ESTABLISHMENT.
POWELL
SMELL
DINING
ROOMS
MODATION
FOR
BED
AND
BREAKFAST
S POWELL
ALDRED & SON
BROAD
ROW

11. GEORGE STREET AND BROAD ROW

The boarding establishment boasts of 'accommodation for motorists' – but cars were still a rare phenomenon in the Yarmouth streets in the early twentieth century. There has recently been a return to the position of a hundred years ago with an increasing number of pedestrian-only streets in the town centre.

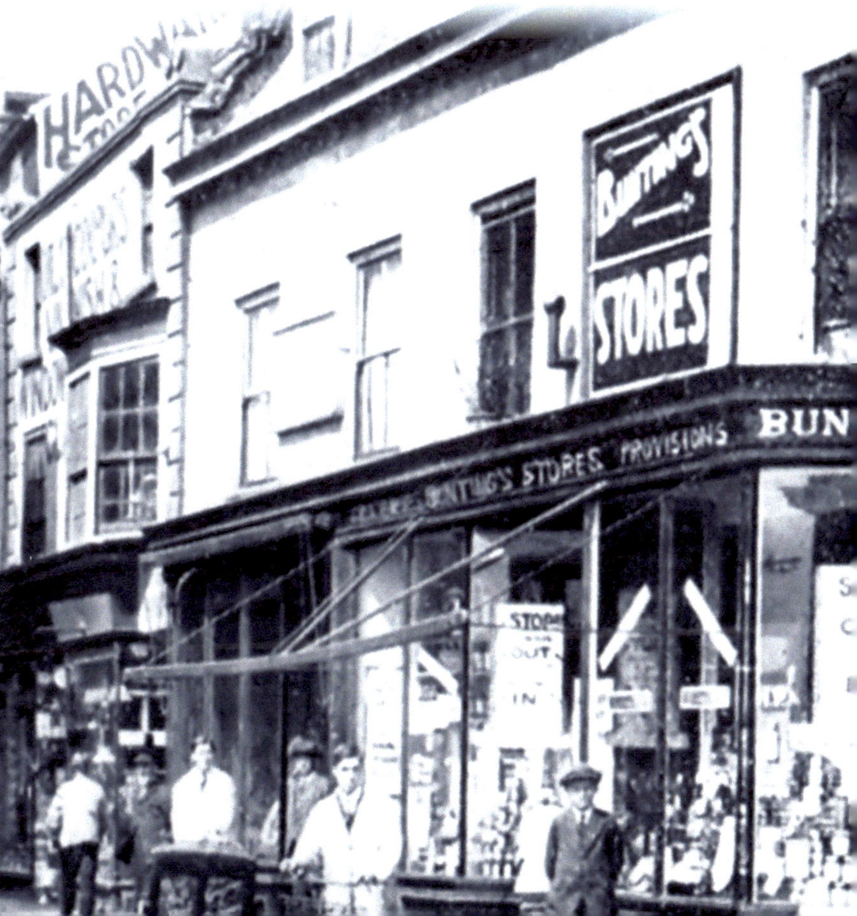

12. YARMOUTH'S GENERAL STORE: PALMERS'

Palmer Brothers have been a major department store for well over a century. In 1897, they advertised: 'The Public are invited to view the Premises, which are now admitted to be the finest in the Eastern Counties, covering a ground space of 16,000 square feet, and absorbing four Front Shops, and twenty-five other properties, and fitted throughout in Natural Woods'.

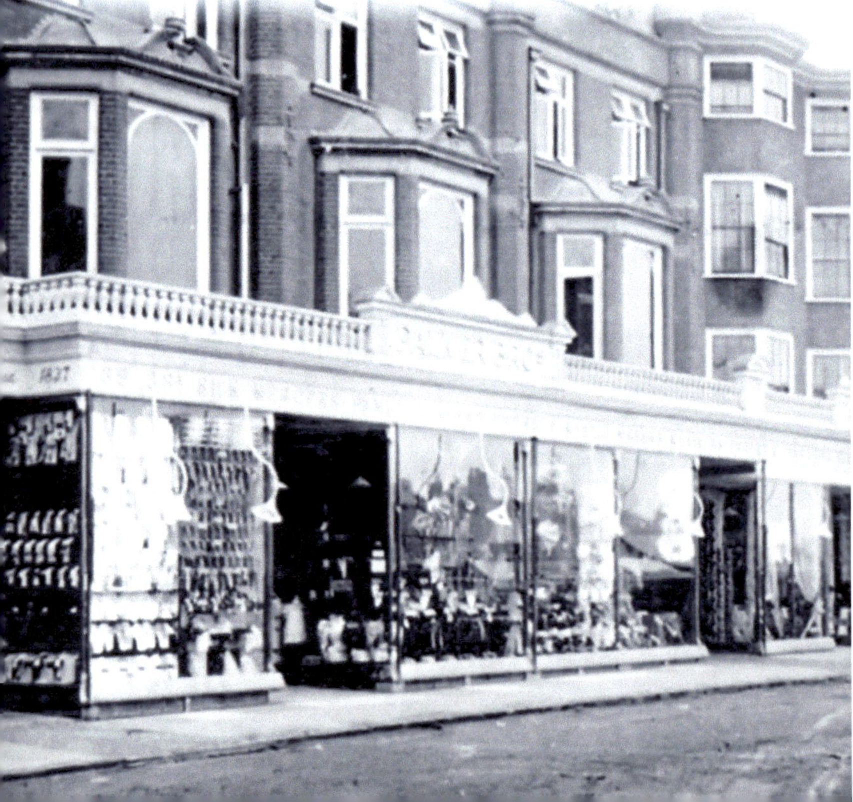

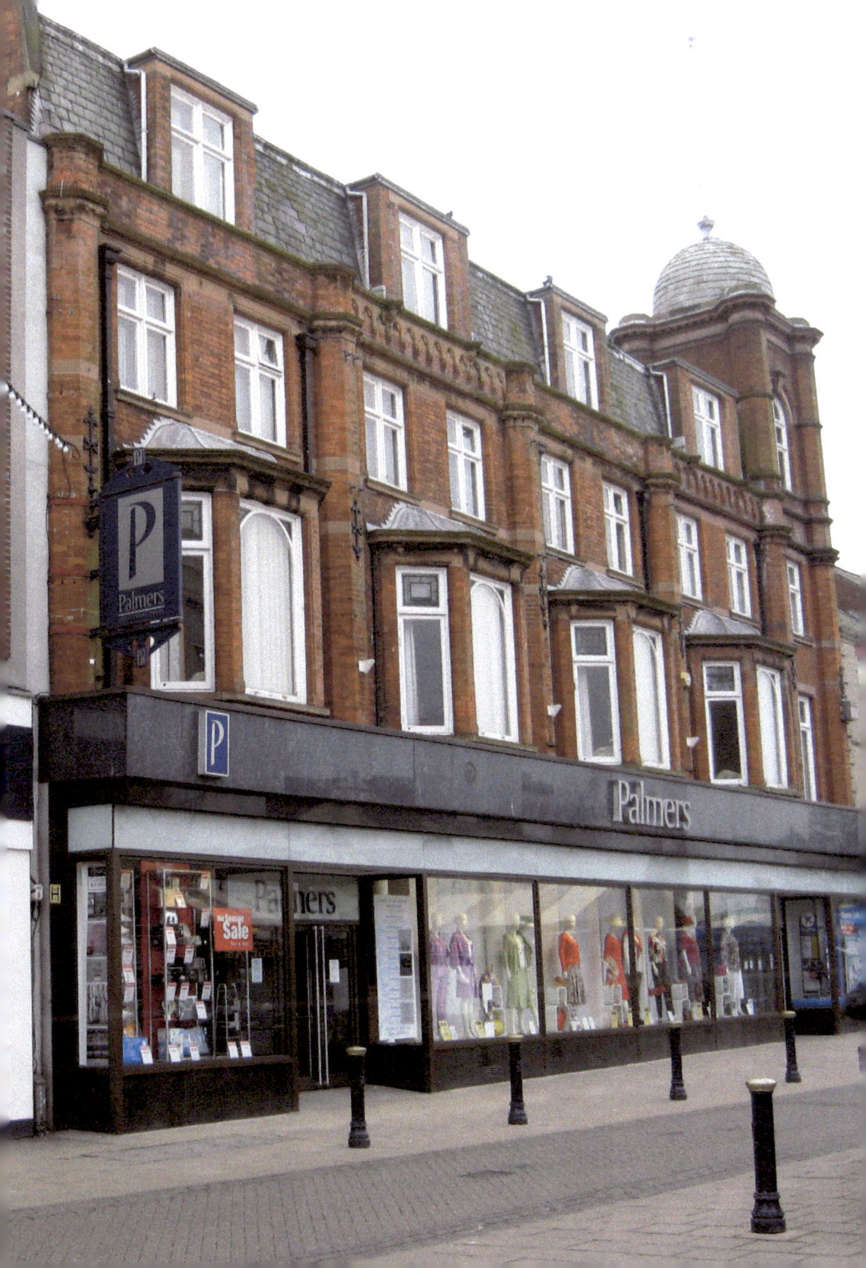

13. SHOPPING AT ARNOLDS'

The Arnold brothers were drapers, and their shop was founded in Yarmouth in 1869. At the time of this photograph, taken in 1897, it boasted a newly-arranged dress department, millinery, mantle and ladies' outfitting show-rooms, as well as a carpet warehouse. The King Street shop was devastated by fire in 1919.

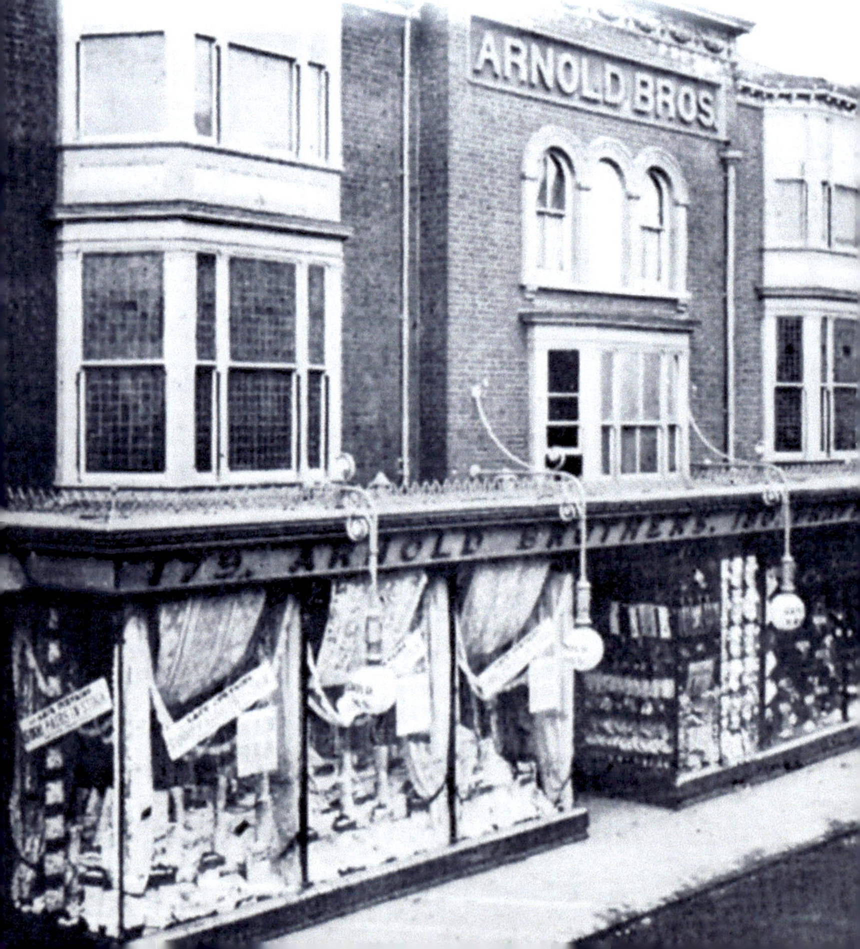

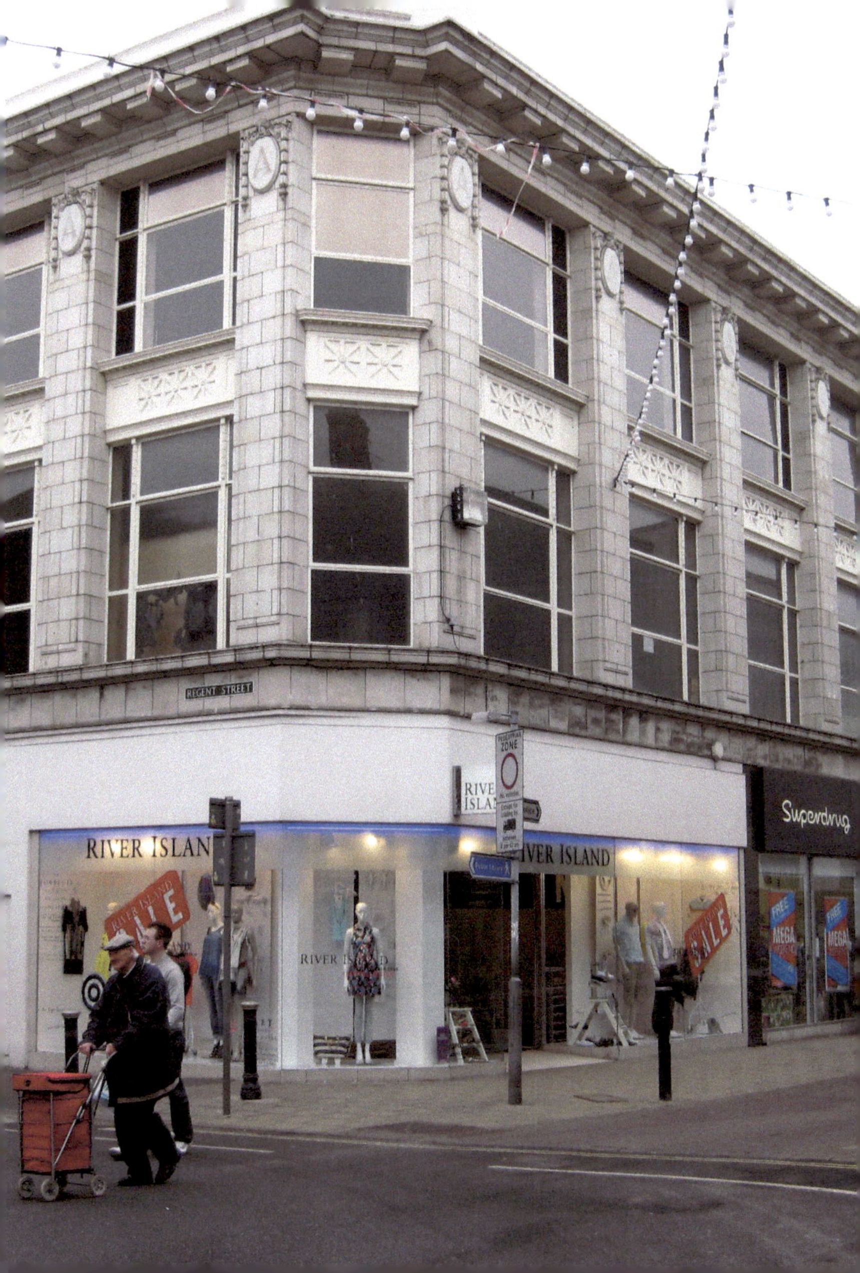
REGENT STREET
RIVER ISLAND
RIVER ISLAND
RIVER ISLAND
RIVER ISLAND
Superdrug
SALE
SALE
FREE MEGA
FREE MEGA
PEDESTRIAN ZONE

14. KING STREET

King Street runs along the central spine of Great Yarmouth, from its highest ground in the Market Place southwards. It has been the town's main shopping street for generations. A visitor from Oxford, John Price, described King Street in 1757 as 'a long handsome street and of a proper width, on each side a range of houses and shops, built with brick in general, sashed, neat and uniform'.

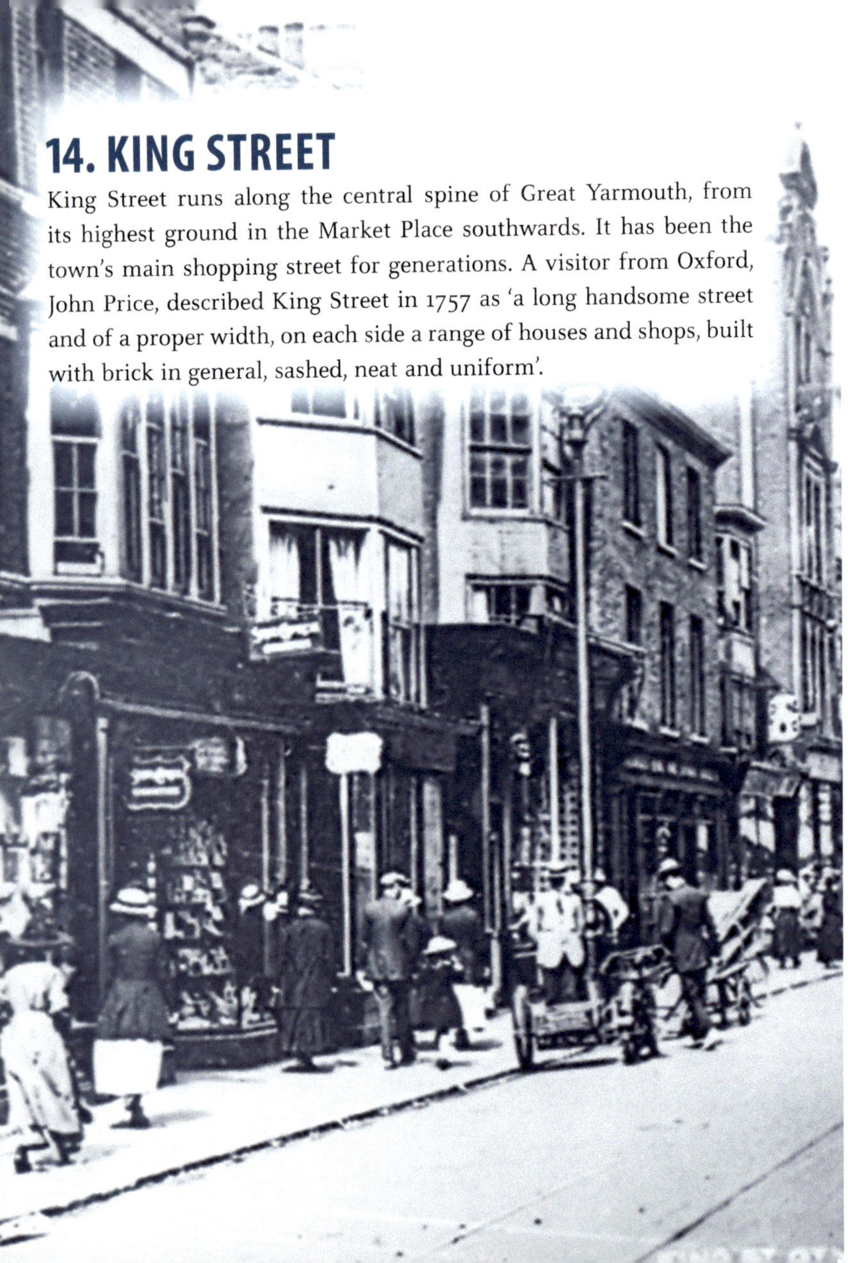

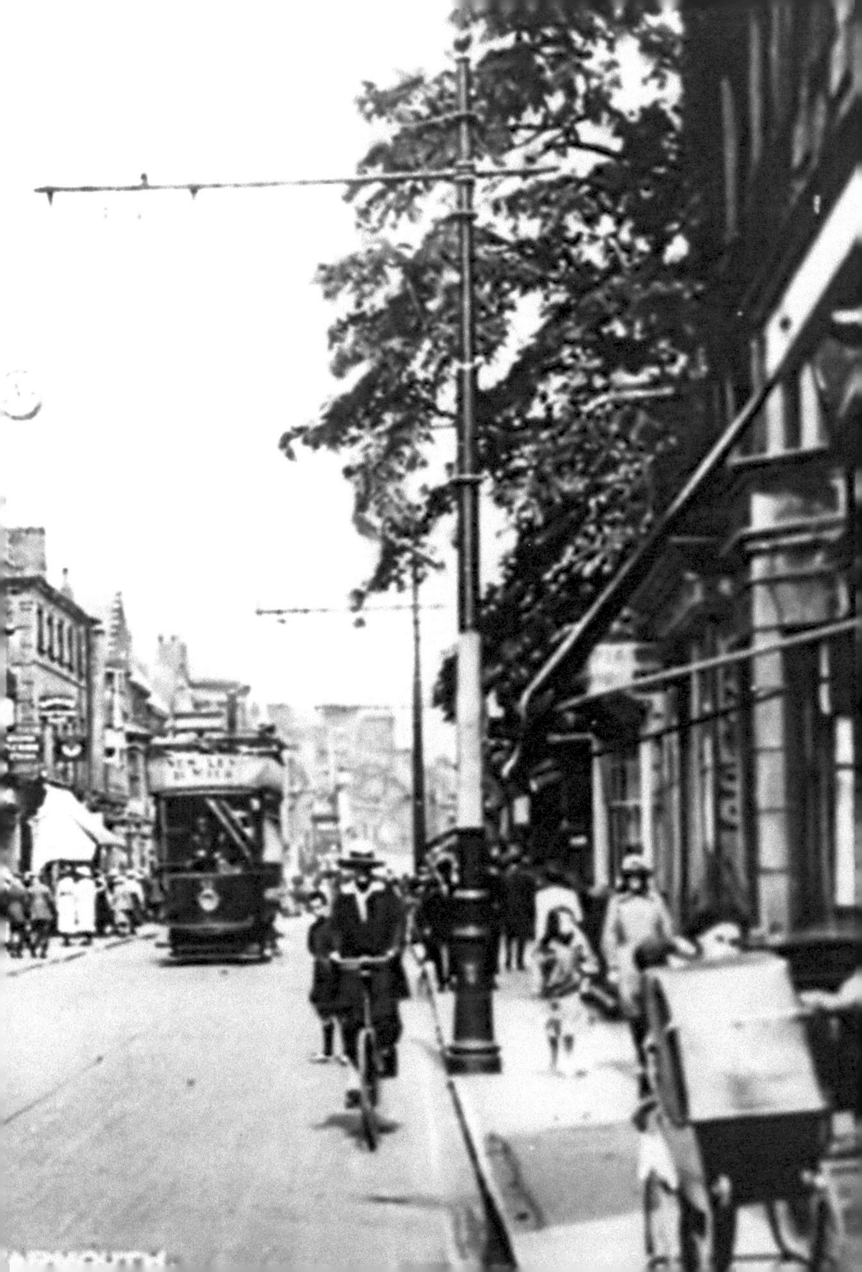
MONMOUTH

15. SAINT GEORGE'S CHAPEL

St George's Chapel was built in 1715 at a cost of £5,861. One hundred years later, the congregation consisted of between 700 and 800 people. By the Second World War, numbers had dwindled and the chapel was closed in the 1950s, the last service being held here on 8 March 1959.

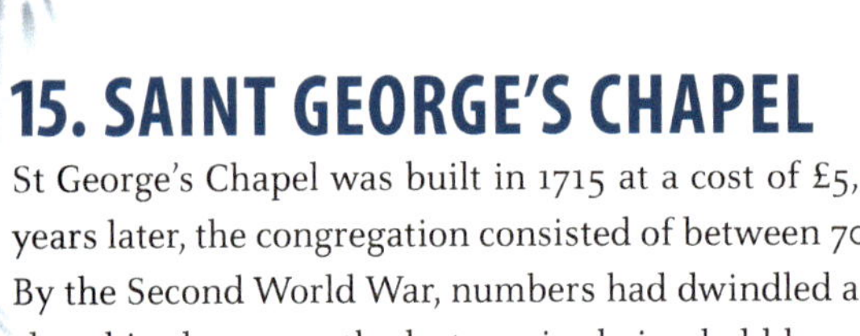

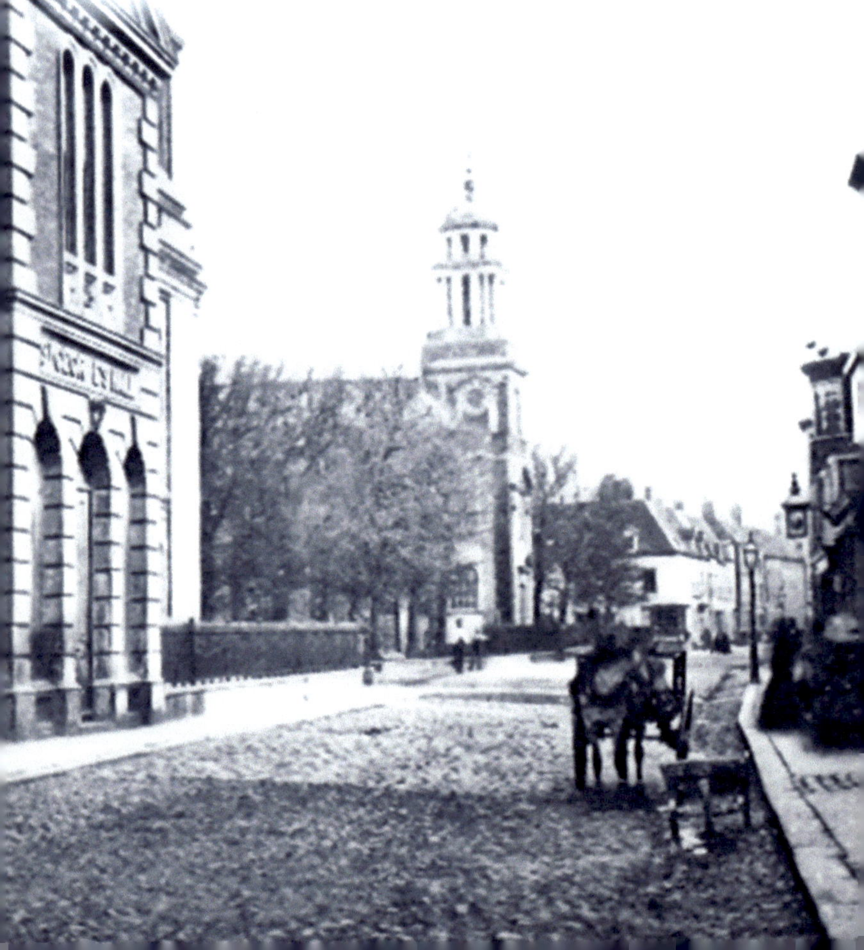

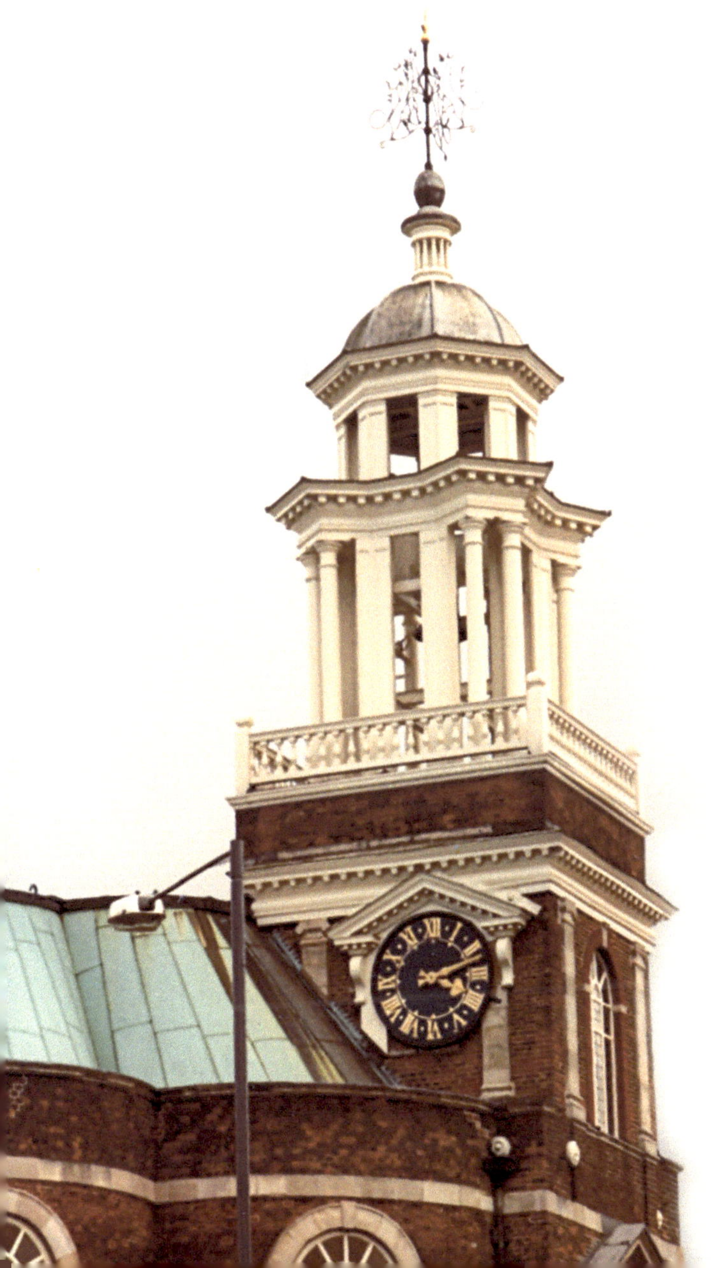

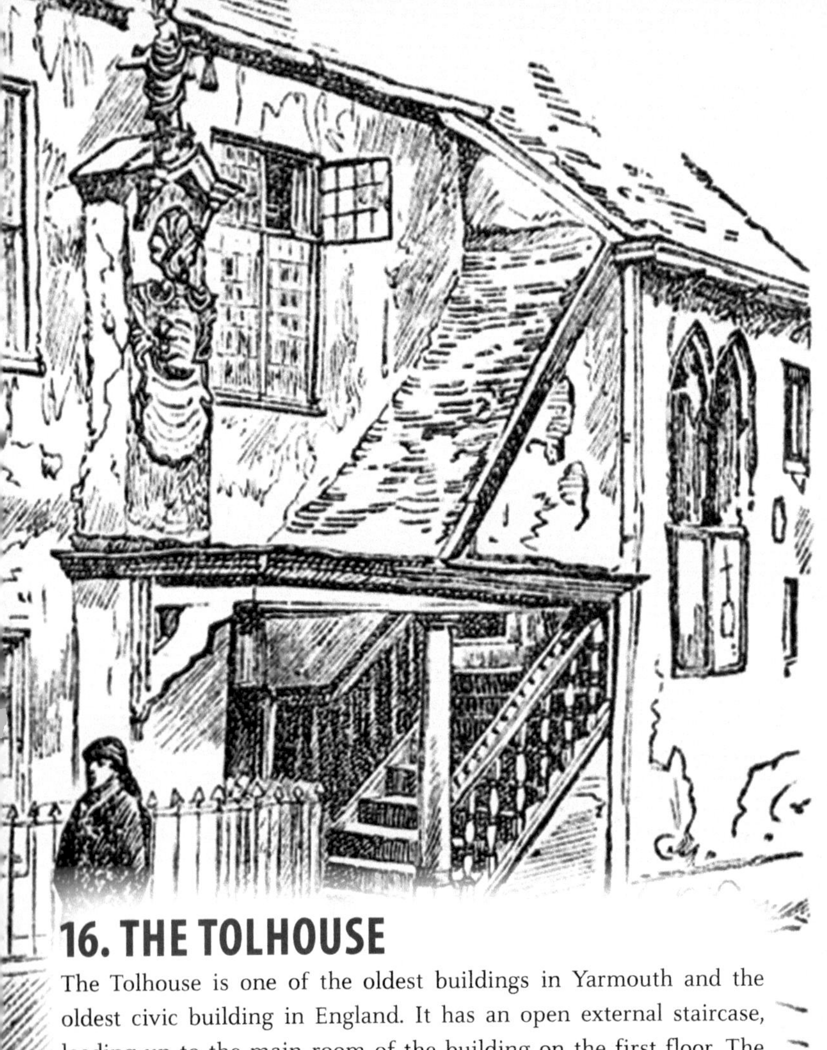

16. THE TOLHOUSE

The Tolhouse is one of the oldest buildings in Yarmouth and the oldest civic building in England. It has an open external staircase, leading up to the main room of the building on the first floor. The common prison was in the basement of the Tolhouse, which is now a museum. The building was badly damaged in the Second World War.

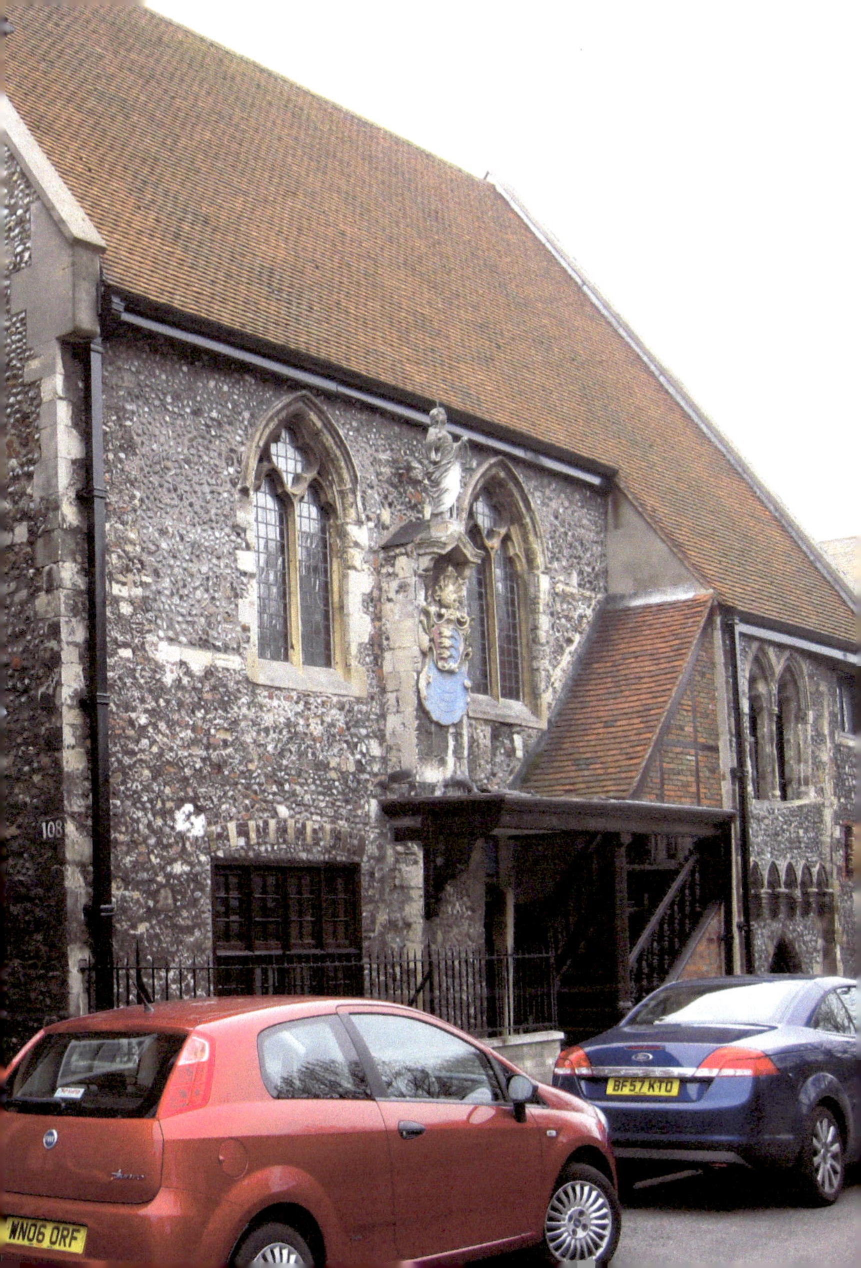

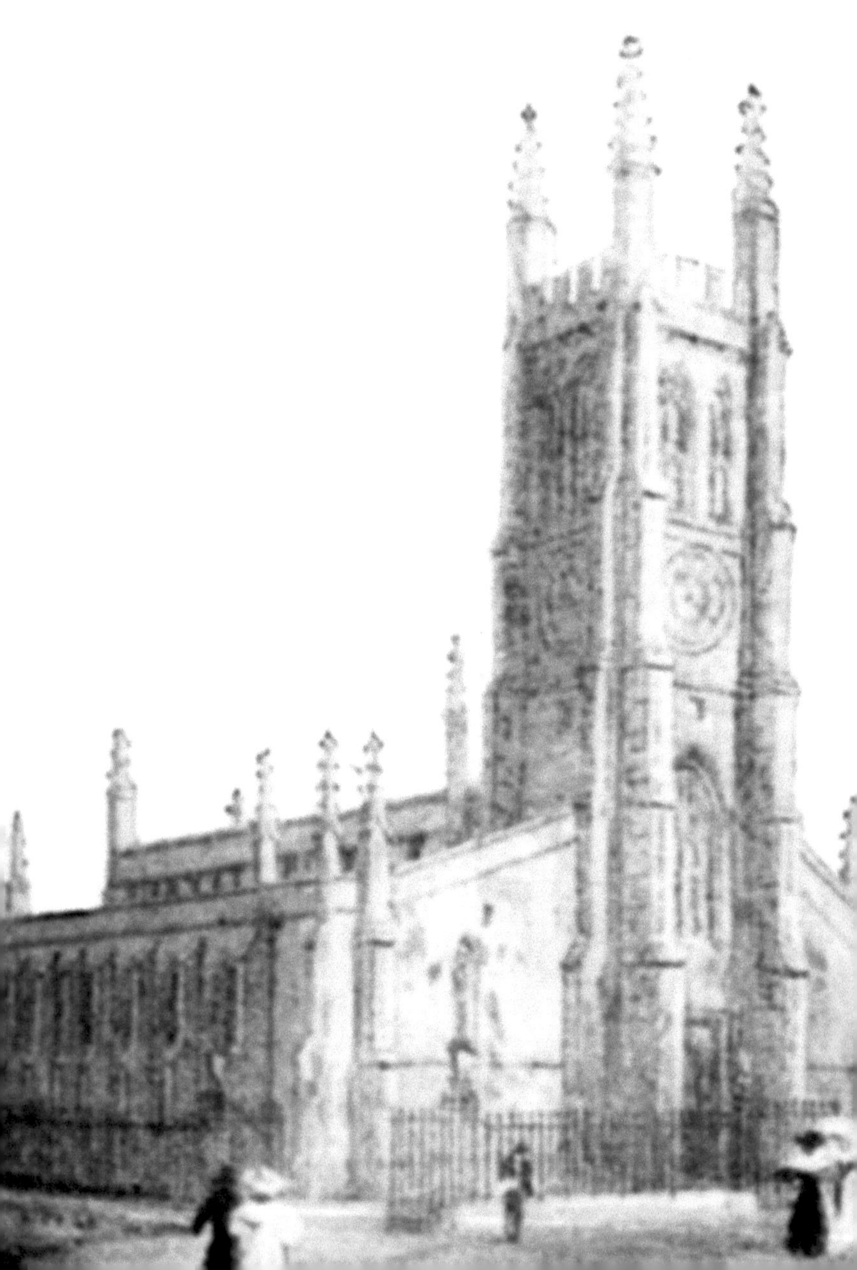

17. SAINT PETER AND SAINT SPIRIDON

The first stone of Saint Peter's church was laid on 7 June 1831. It was designed to hold 1,800 people and cost £12,000. It is now used by the Greek Orthodox community in the town and dedicated to Saint Spiridon. The Greeks, mainly from Cyprus, have added a welcome diversity to the modern town.

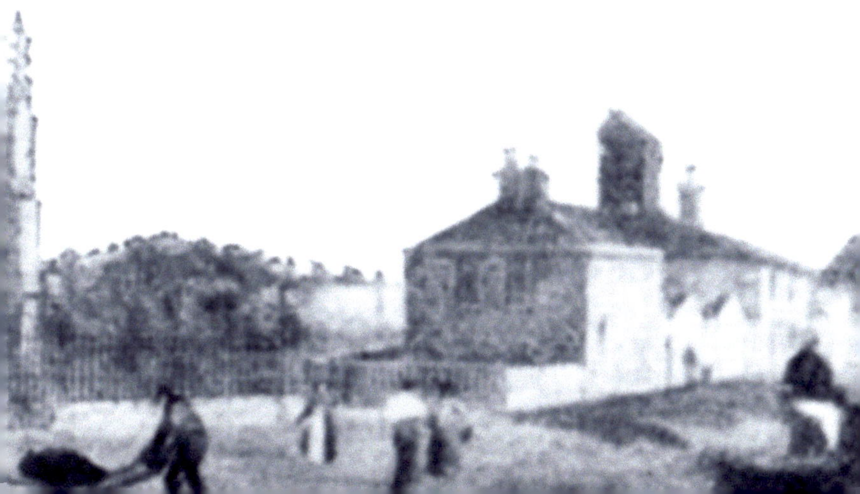

18. THE SOUTH-EAST TOWER

The chequer-board pattern on this tower, in brick and flint, is a striking decorative feature and one that was repeated on the South Gate of the town; the gate was pulled down at the end of the eighteenth century. This tower is only a very short distance from the Time and Tide Museum.

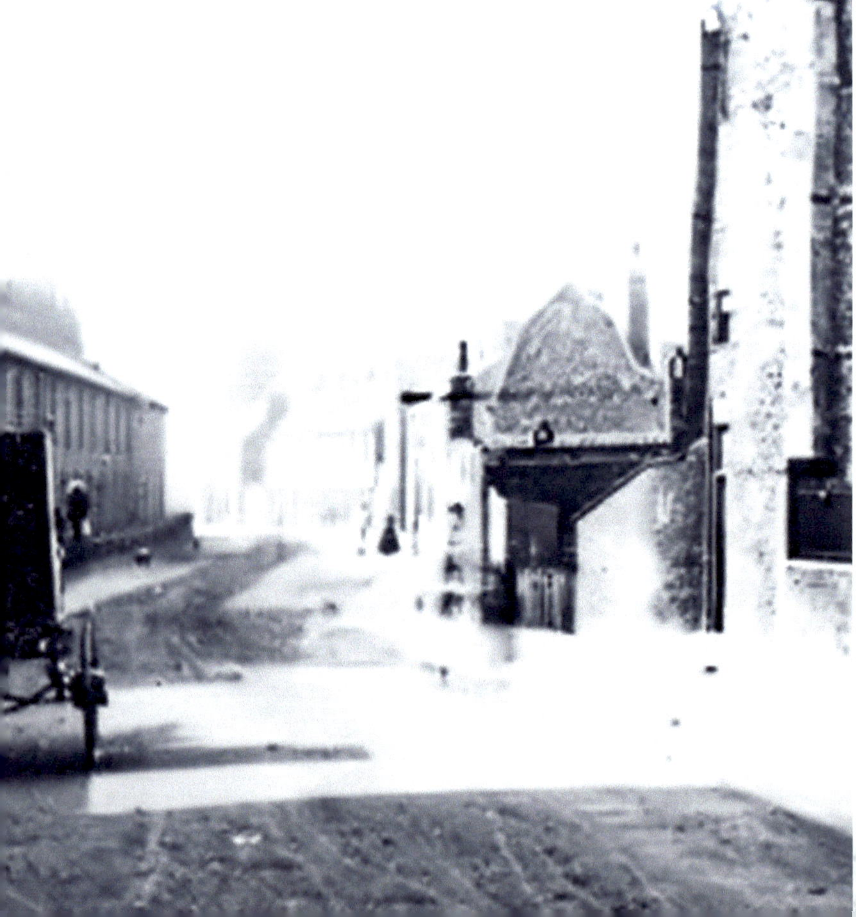

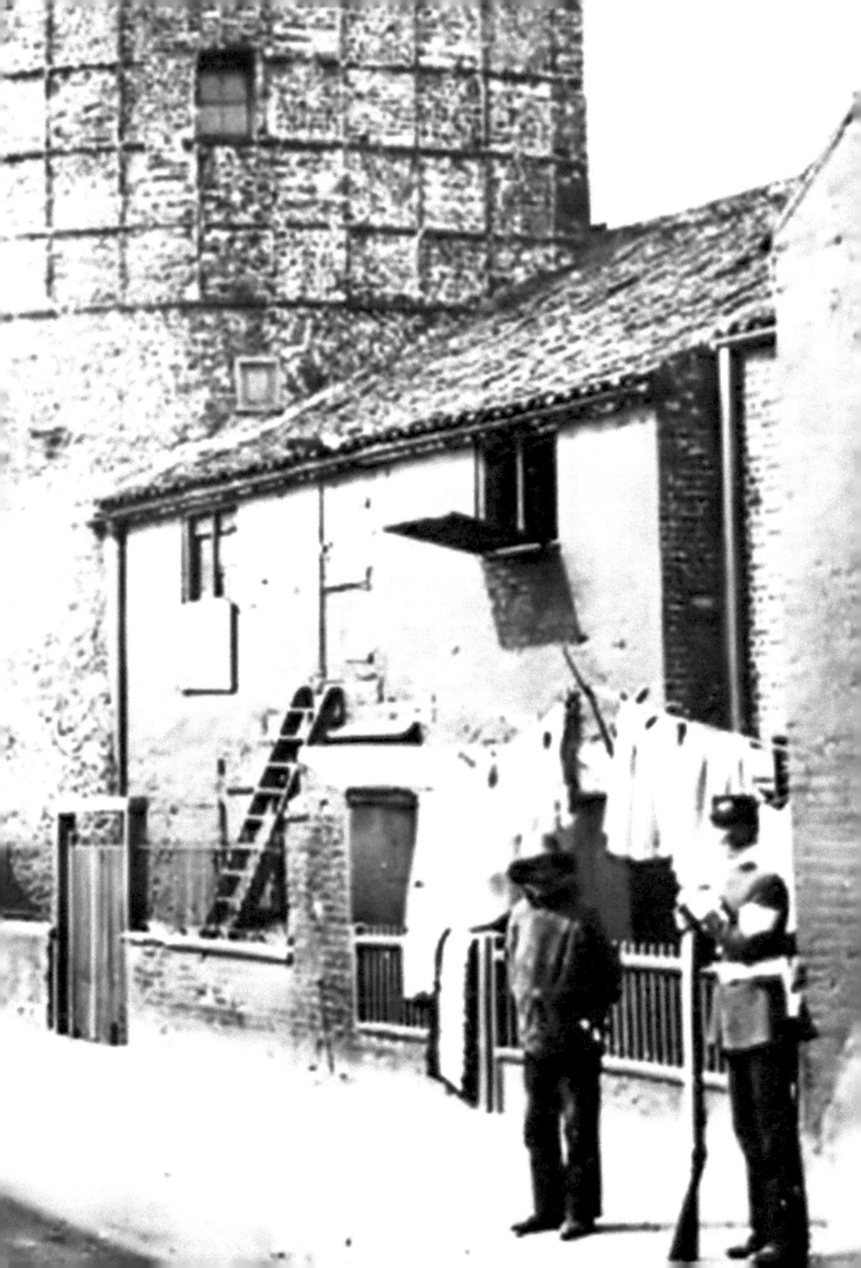

19. BLACKFRIARS TOWER

As long as the town walls were thought necessary for defence, every effort was made to stop people building houses beside them, but by the nineteenth century many buildings had been erected against the walls. Most have been pulled down to show the town walls in all of their glory – one of the finest surviving urban defences in England, and little known to the many thousands of summer visitors to the town.

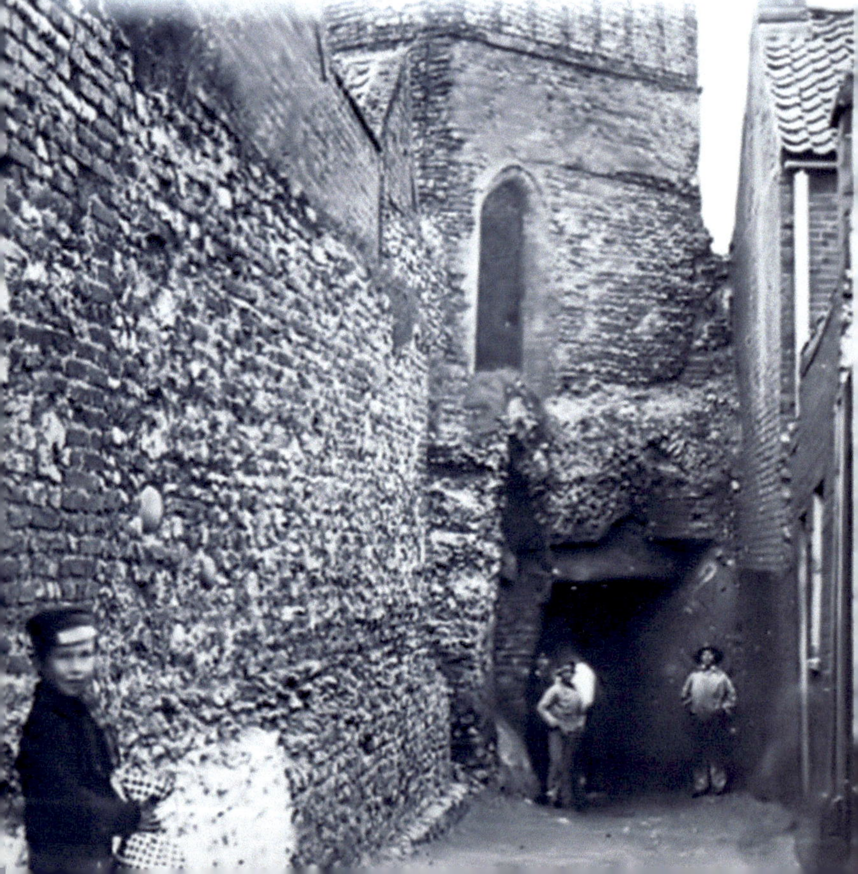

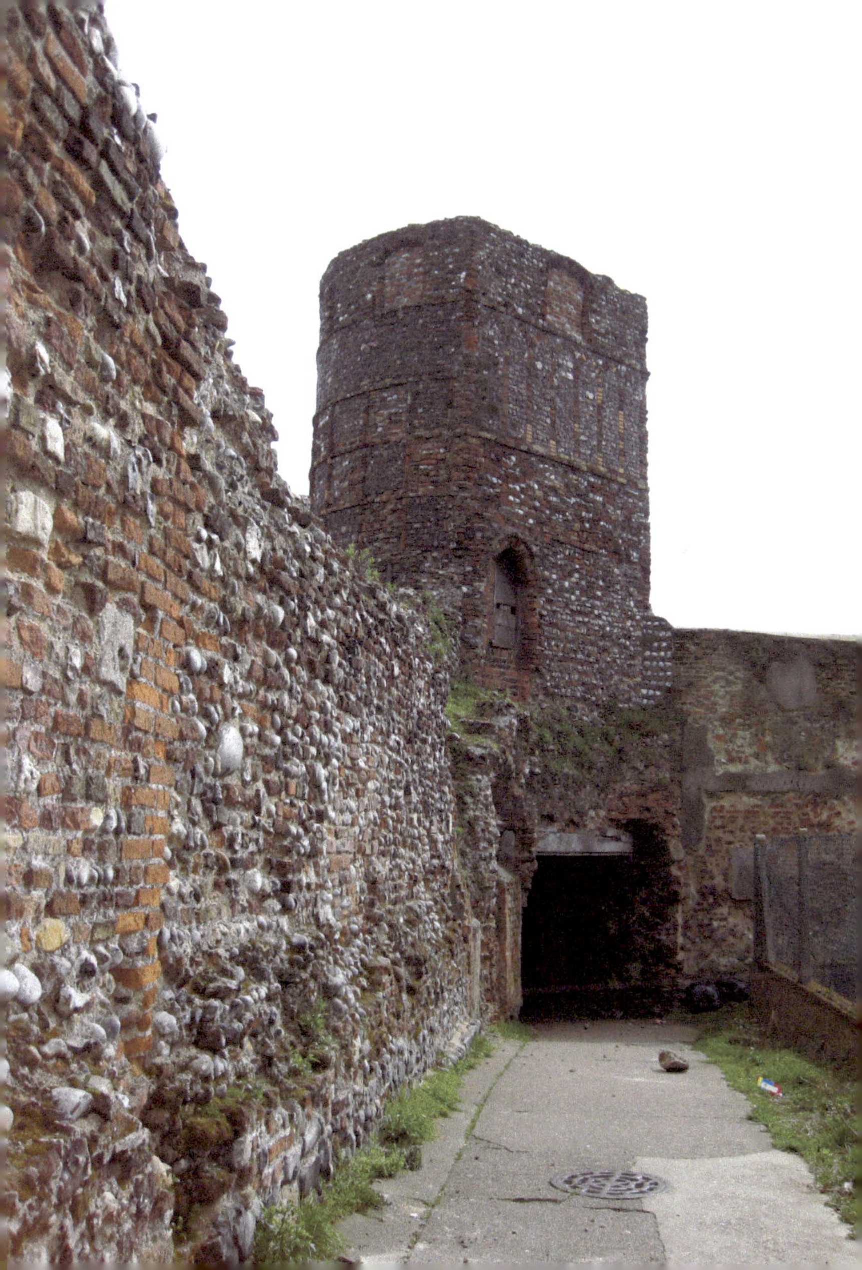

The Pleasure Beach, Gt. Yarmouth

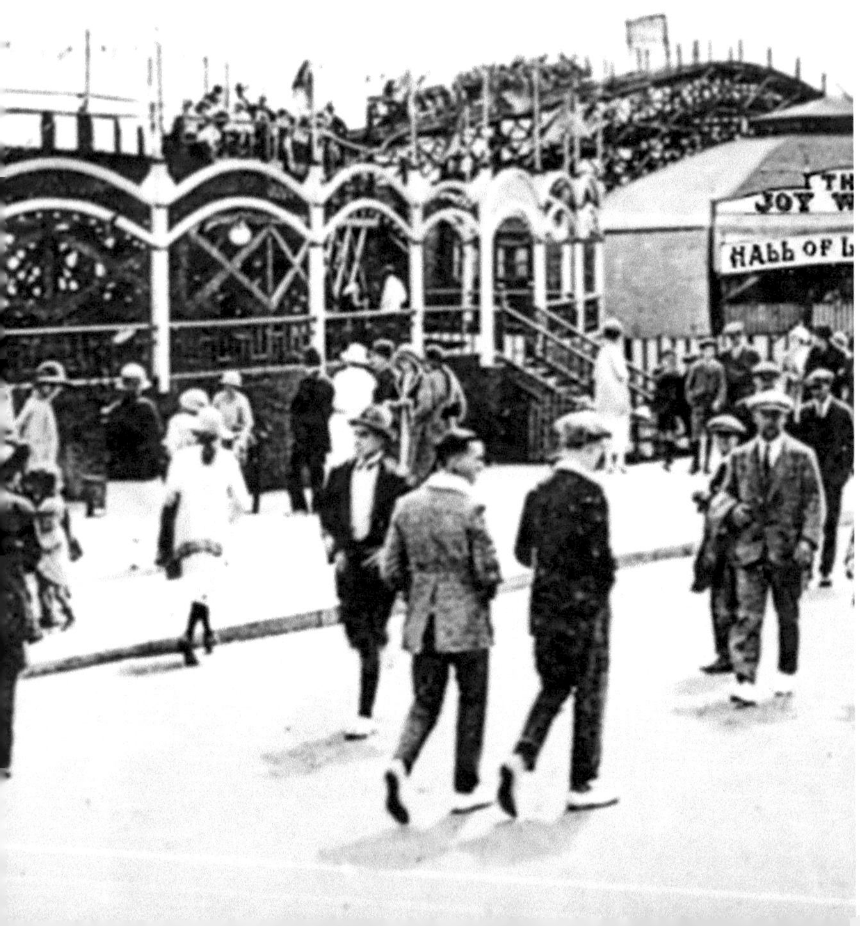

20. ALL THE FUN OF THE FAIR

As the *Ward Lock Guide* of 1906 says, 'From sunrise to sunset there is no time to be dull in merry, moving, whirling Yarmouth, and indoor entertainments to keep the ball rolling when the stars look down upon the deserted sands'. This is just as true over a century later – and long may it continue. Yarmouth needs its visitors and knows how to make them welcome.

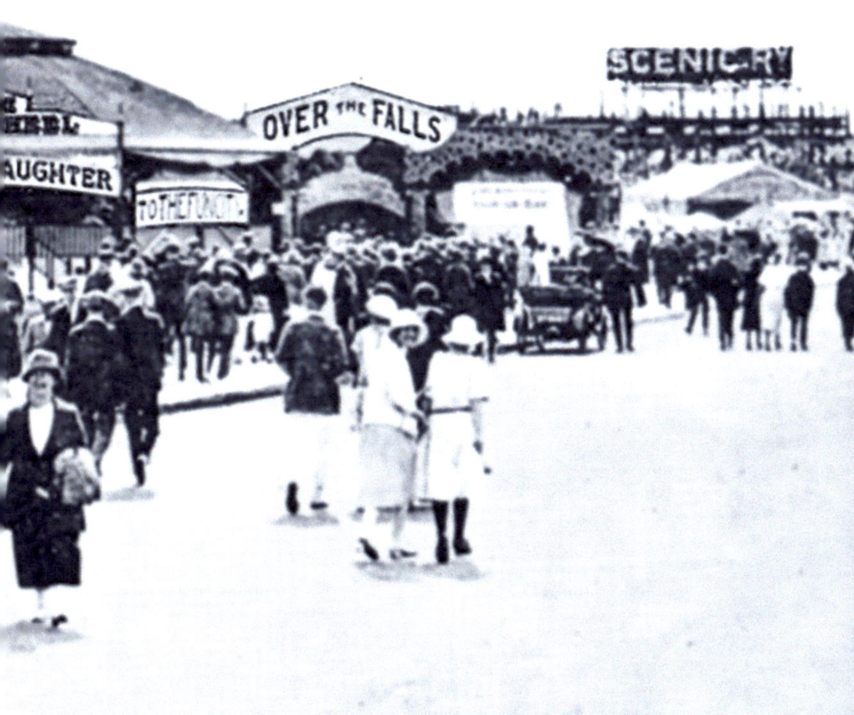

Wellington Pier Gardens, Gt. Yarmouth

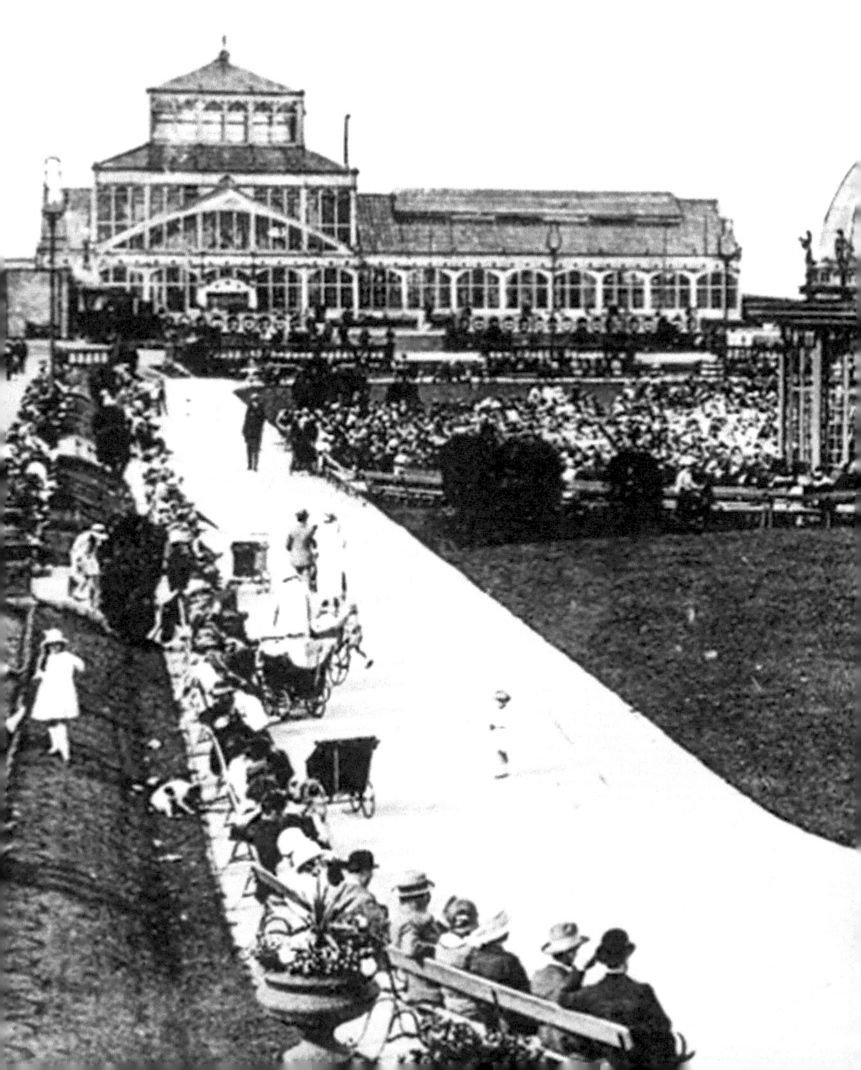

21. SOUTH OF THE WELLINGTON PIER

The bandstand in Wellington Gardens was a most attractive feature: it had a series of statues of muses along the top, young women, each playing a different musical instrument. It was demolished in the Second World War. The model village and crazy golf course now stand on its site.

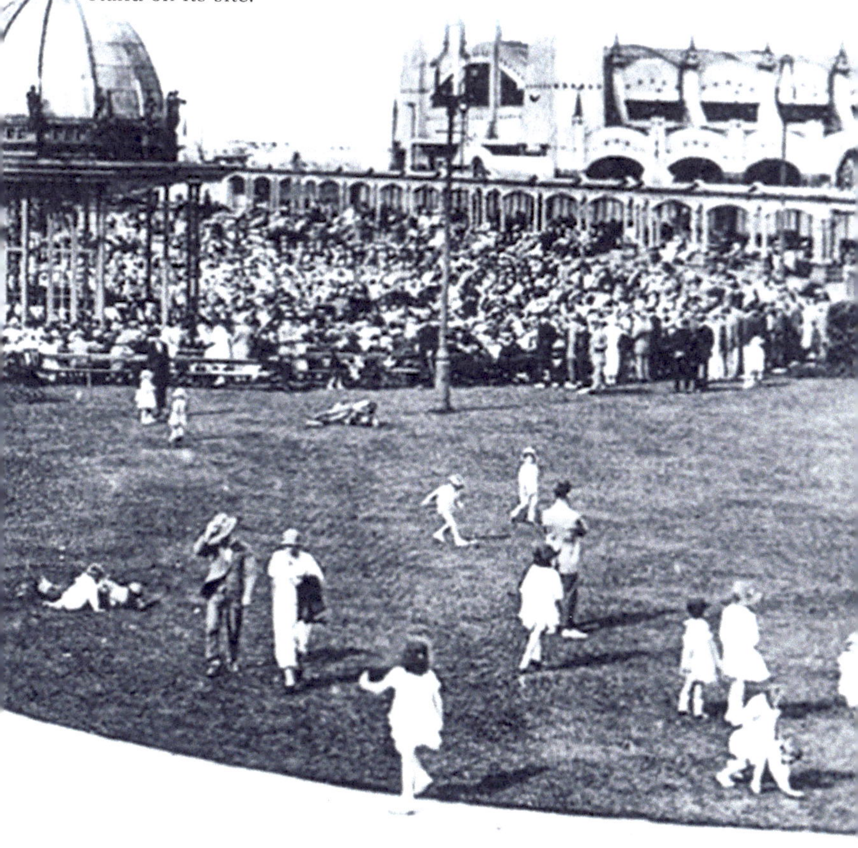

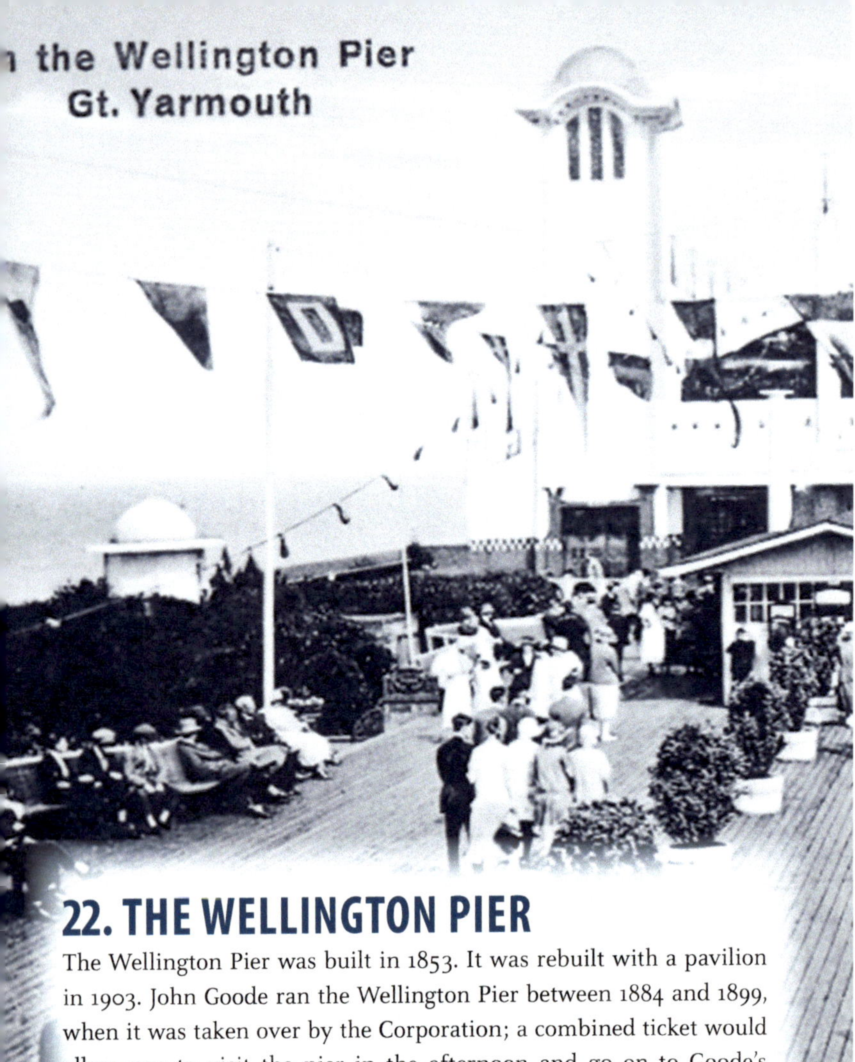

22. THE WELLINGTON PIER

The Wellington Pier was built in 1853. It was rebuilt with a pavilion in 1903. John Goode ran the Wellington Pier between 1884 and 1899, when it was taken over by the Corporation; a combined ticket would allow you to visit the pier in the afternoon and go on to Goode's dancing establishment at Winton's Rooms in the evening. The pier was bought by the Corporation in 1900.

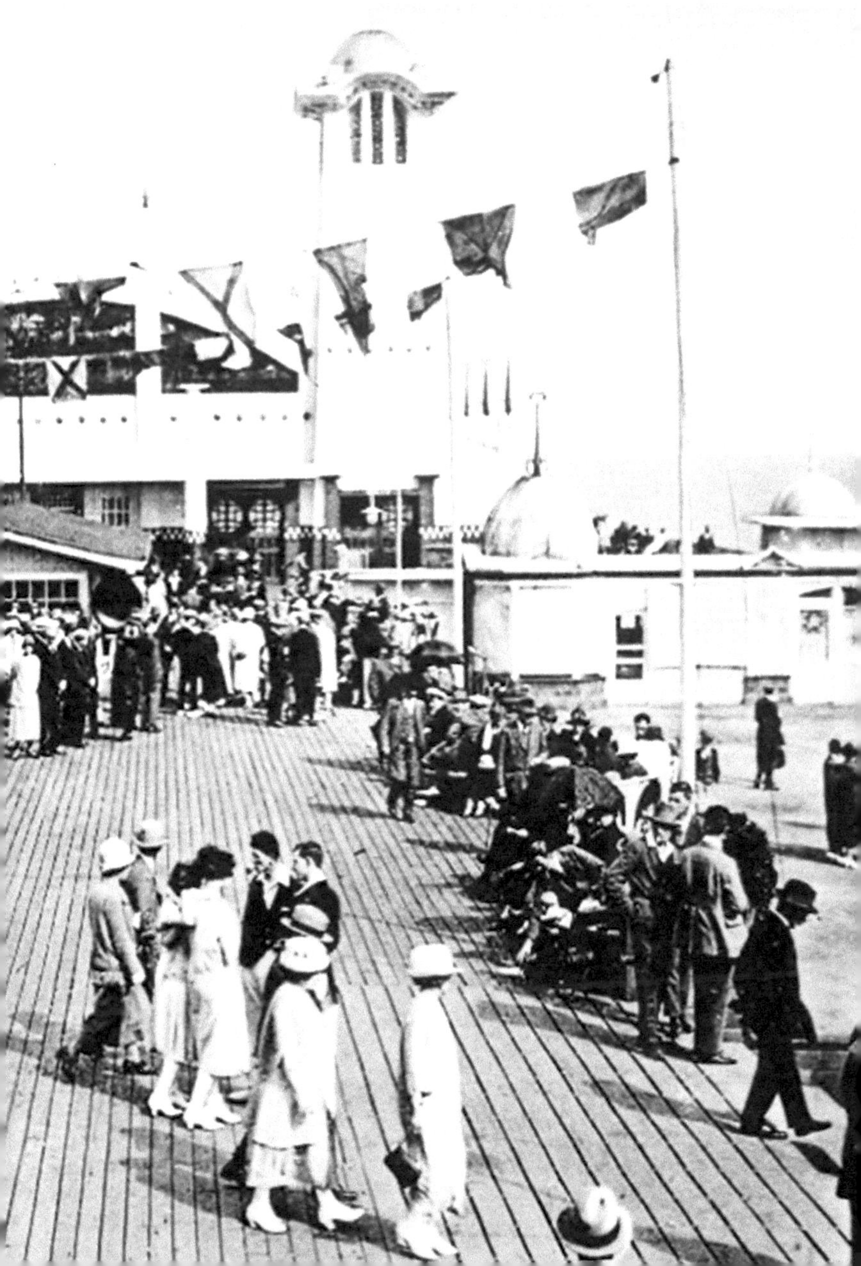

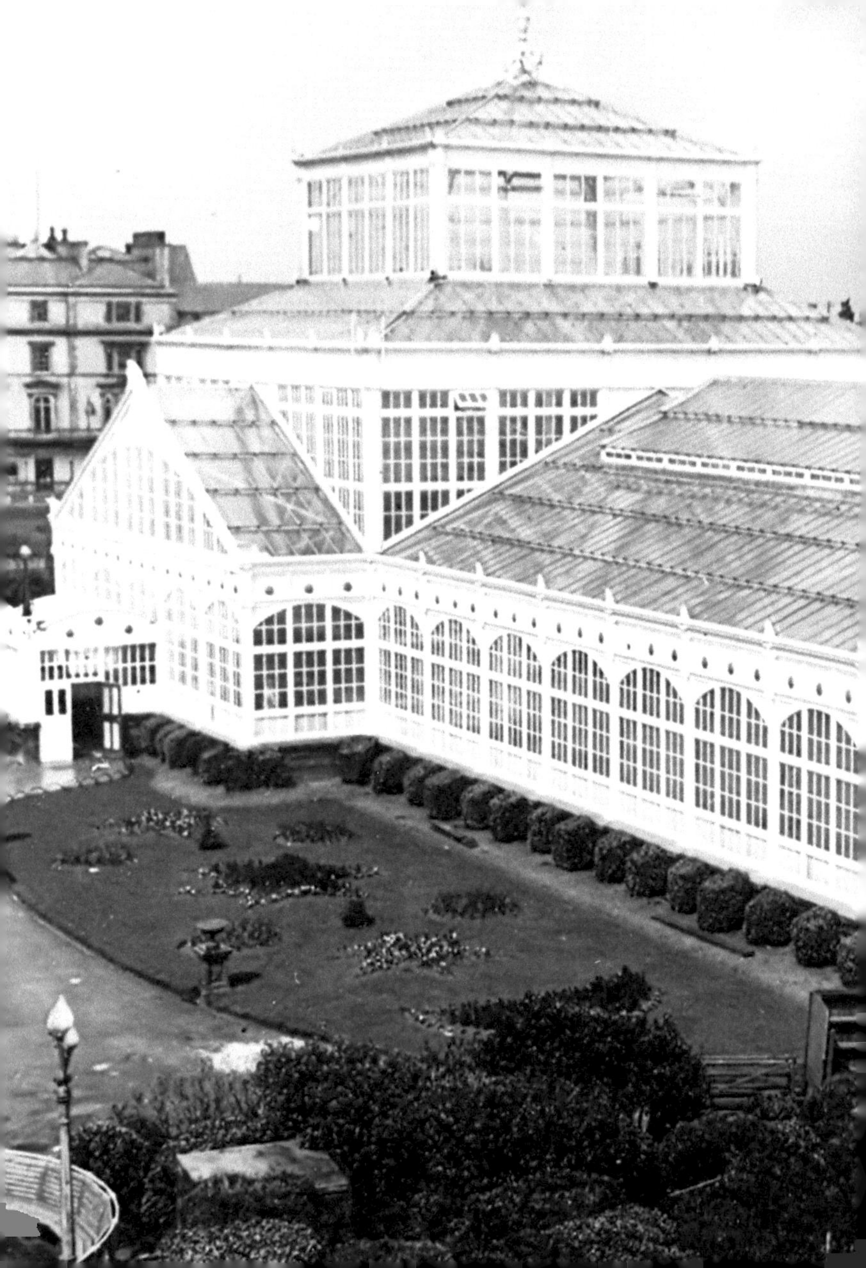

23. A PRESENT FROM TORQUAY – THE WINTER GARDENS

The Winter Gardens was originally built in Torquay in 1878–91. It was transported to Yarmouth and re-erected in 1903; they paid £1,300 for it, just one tenth of its original cost, but it must have been difficult and costly to transport across the entire width of England! However, it has certainly paid for itself many times over as a place to go on a wet and cold Yarmouth day. It has had many uses: at one time it was used as a skating rink, and later as a German-style beer cellar.

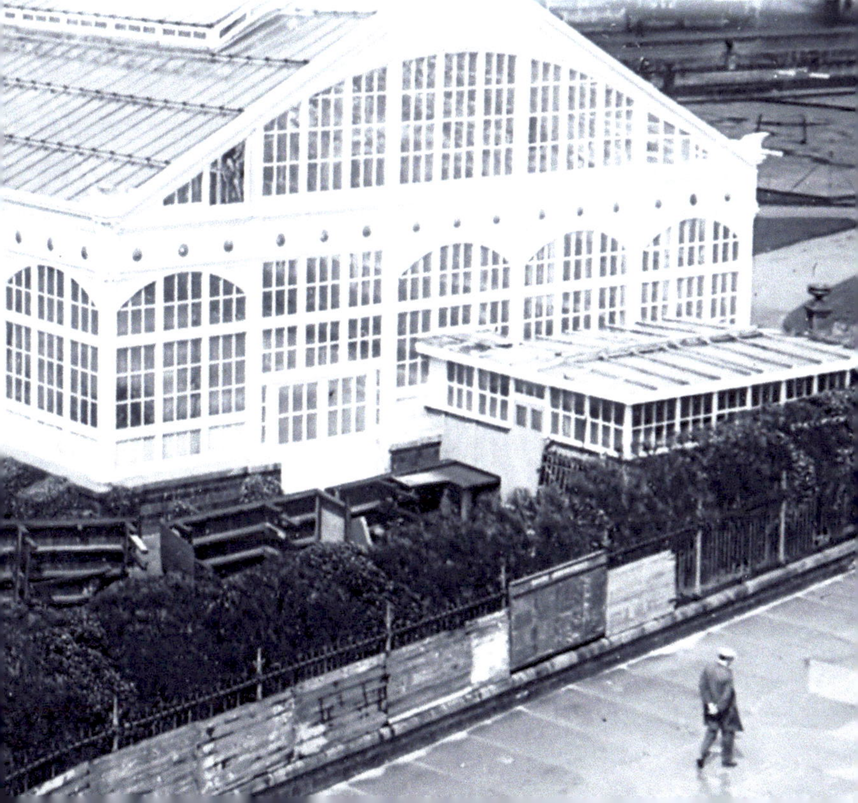

24. THE BATHING MACHINE

A century ago, the bathing machine was an essential element of beach equipment, allowing people to change in privacy – and to plunge directly into the water from the machine. In the early years, there were separate areas of beach reserved for men's and women's machines. Modesty ruled: even men had at all times to be covered 'from neck to knee'!

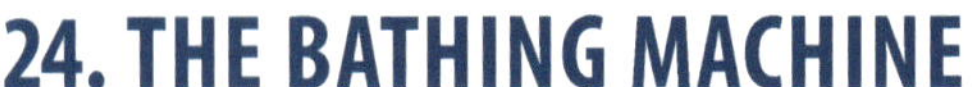

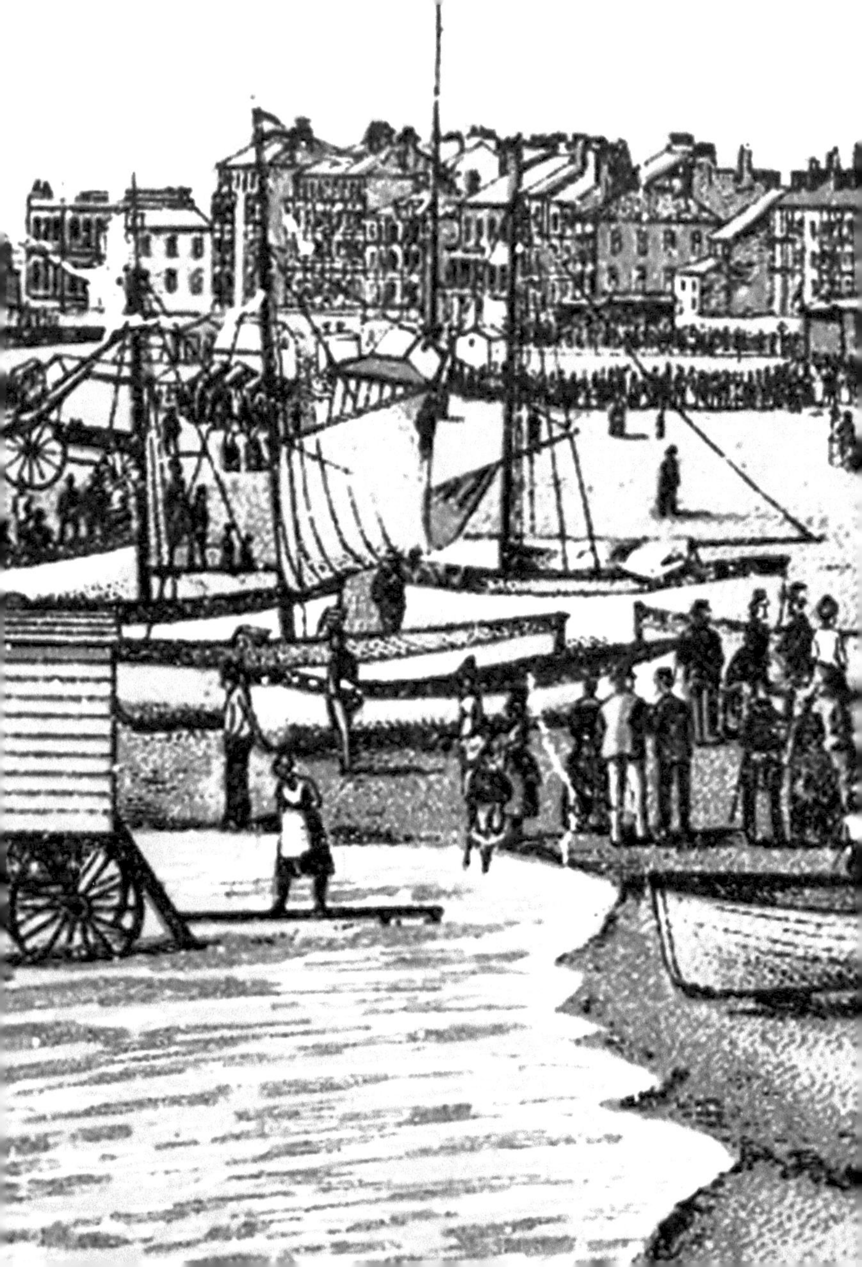

25. UNDERNEATH THE ARCHES

These arches across the streets are not as well known to Yarmouth people as they might be. They reflect an era of a century and a half ago, when the Victoria Building Co. of Great Yarmouth was trying to develop this part of the seafront for high-class housing. The Arches were built in 1846 and 1847, and the larger one, known as the Wellington Arch, was intended as the grand entrance to the estate.

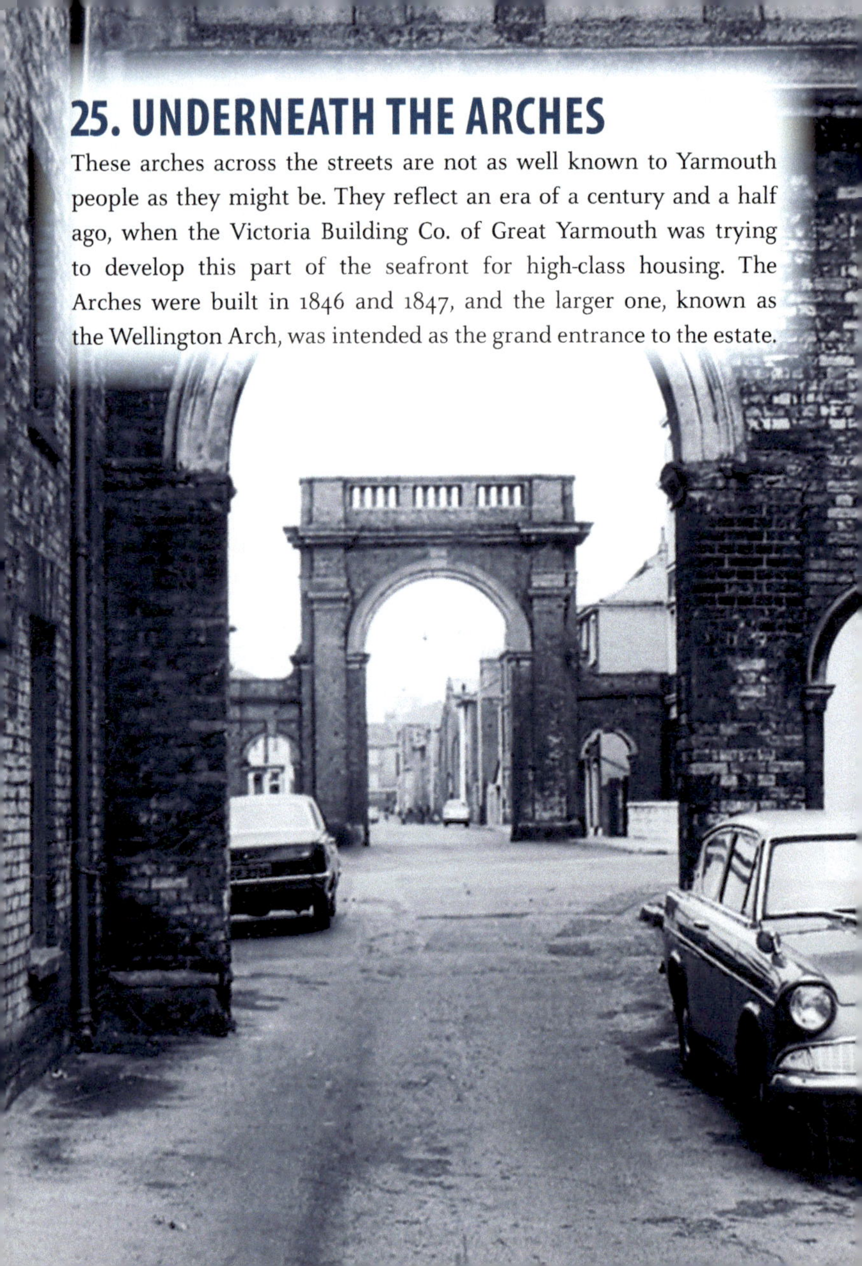

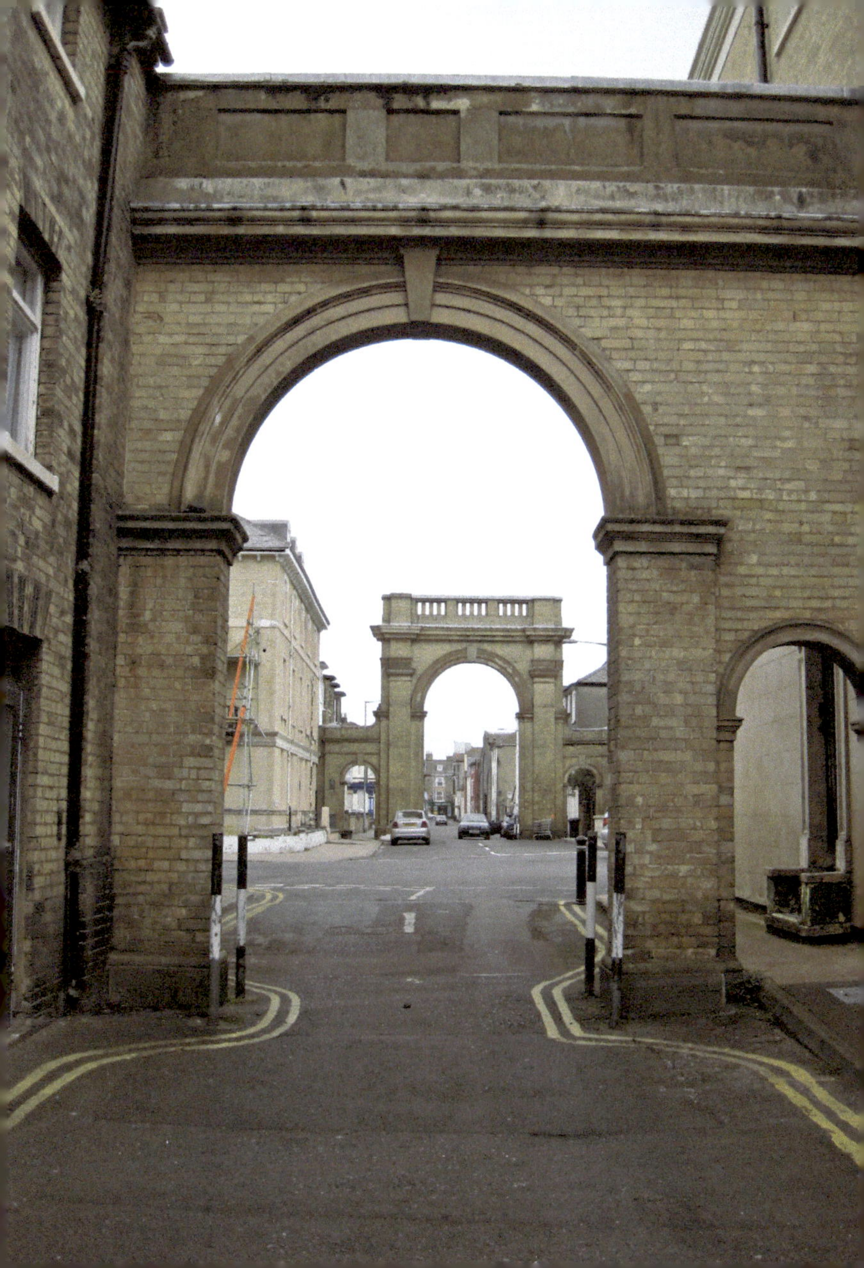

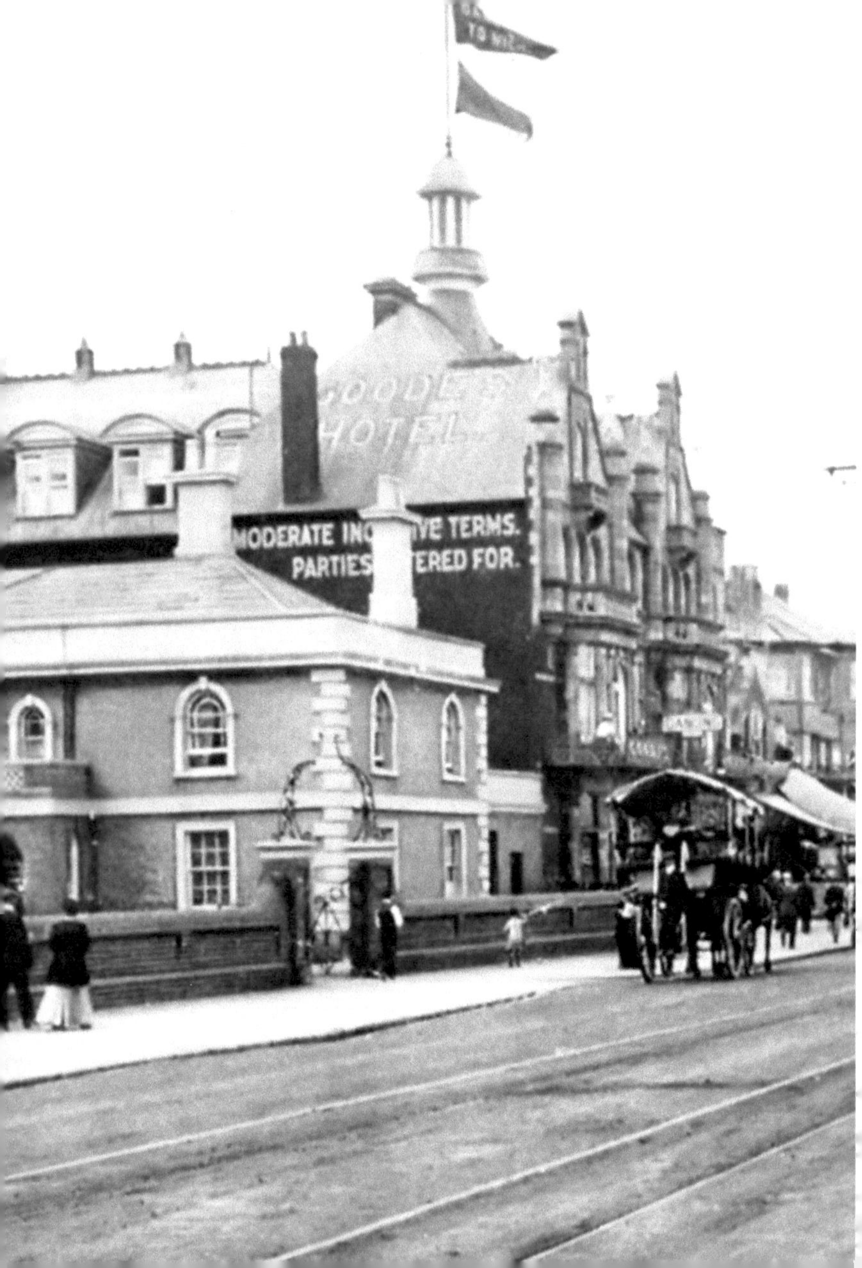
GOODE'S
HOTEL
MODERATE INCLUSIVE TERMS.
PARTIES CATERED FOR.

26. GOODE'S HOTEL

Goode's Hotel and ballroom opened in July 1902, on the site of Winton's Rooms, a dancing academy that had been destroyed by fire on the evening of 5 September 1901 and which had been owned by John Goode and his brother from about 1896. Edward Winton's name could be seen in the coloured glass over one of the doors until 1972. The Tower Hotel next door was built in 1964.

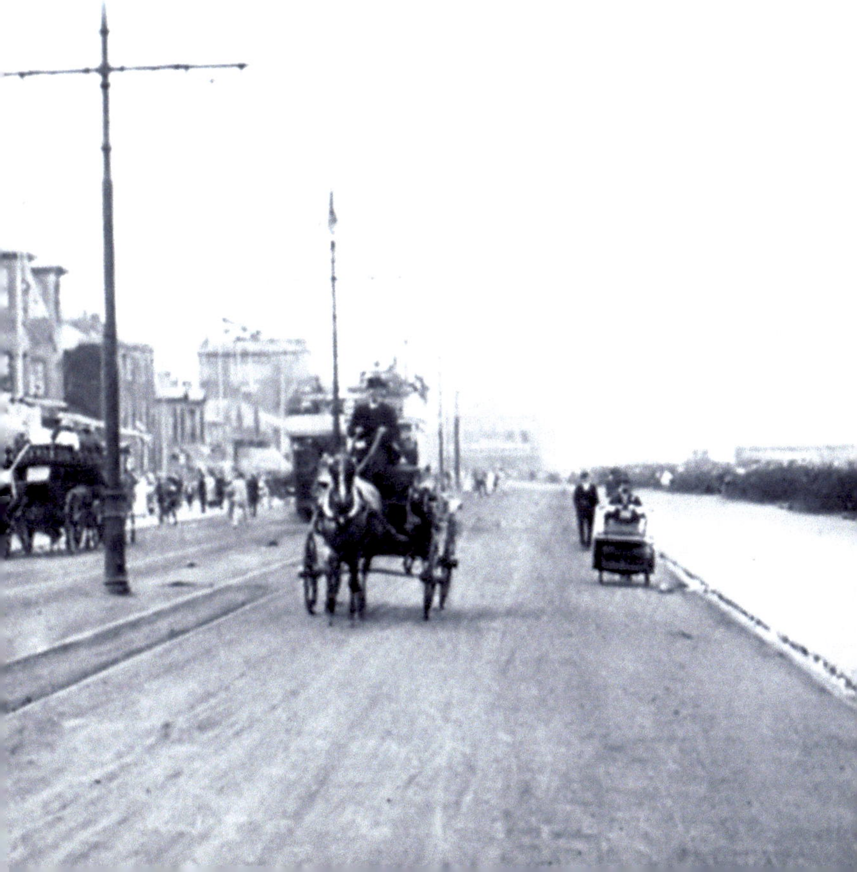

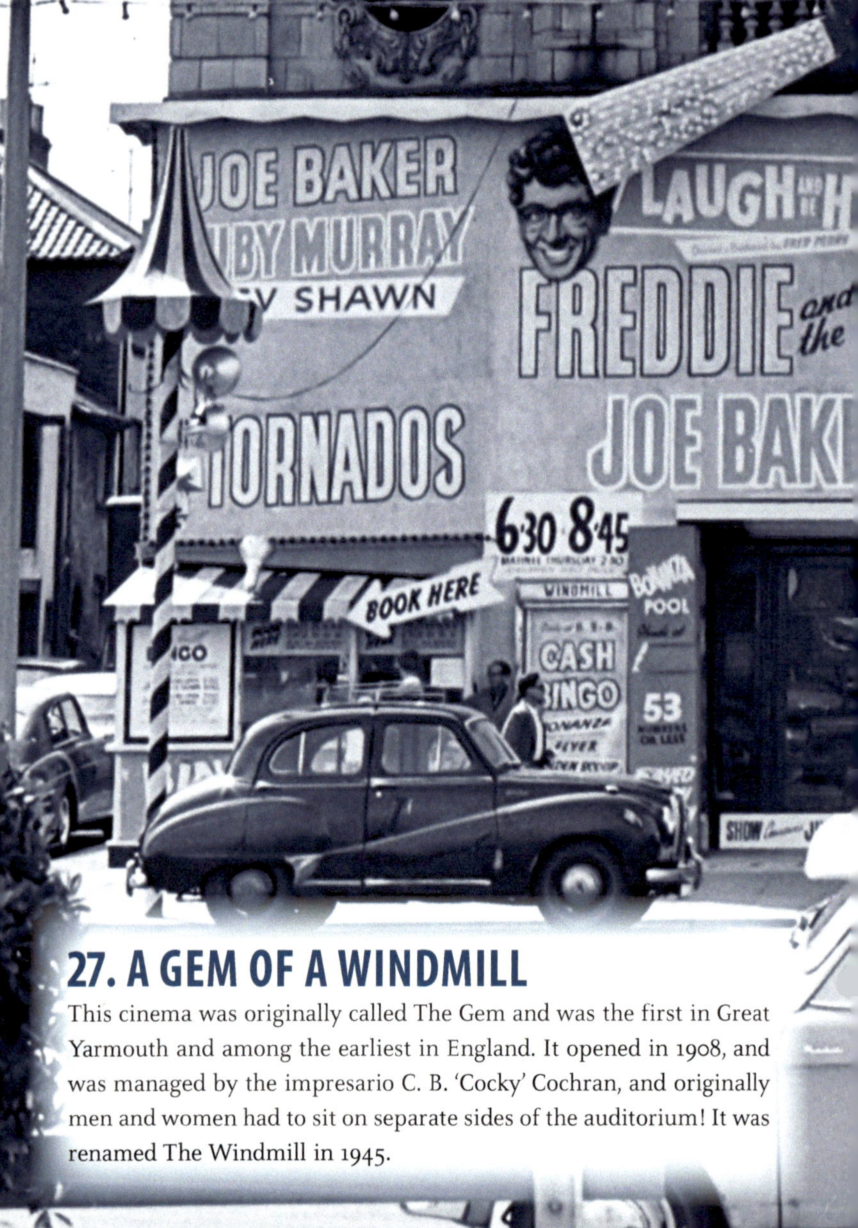

27. A GEM OF A WINDMILL

This cinema was originally called The Gem and was the first in Great Yarmouth and among the earliest in England. It opened in 1908, and was managed by the impresario C. B. 'Cocky' Cochran, and originally men and women had to sit on separate sides of the auditorium! It was renamed The Windmill in 1945.

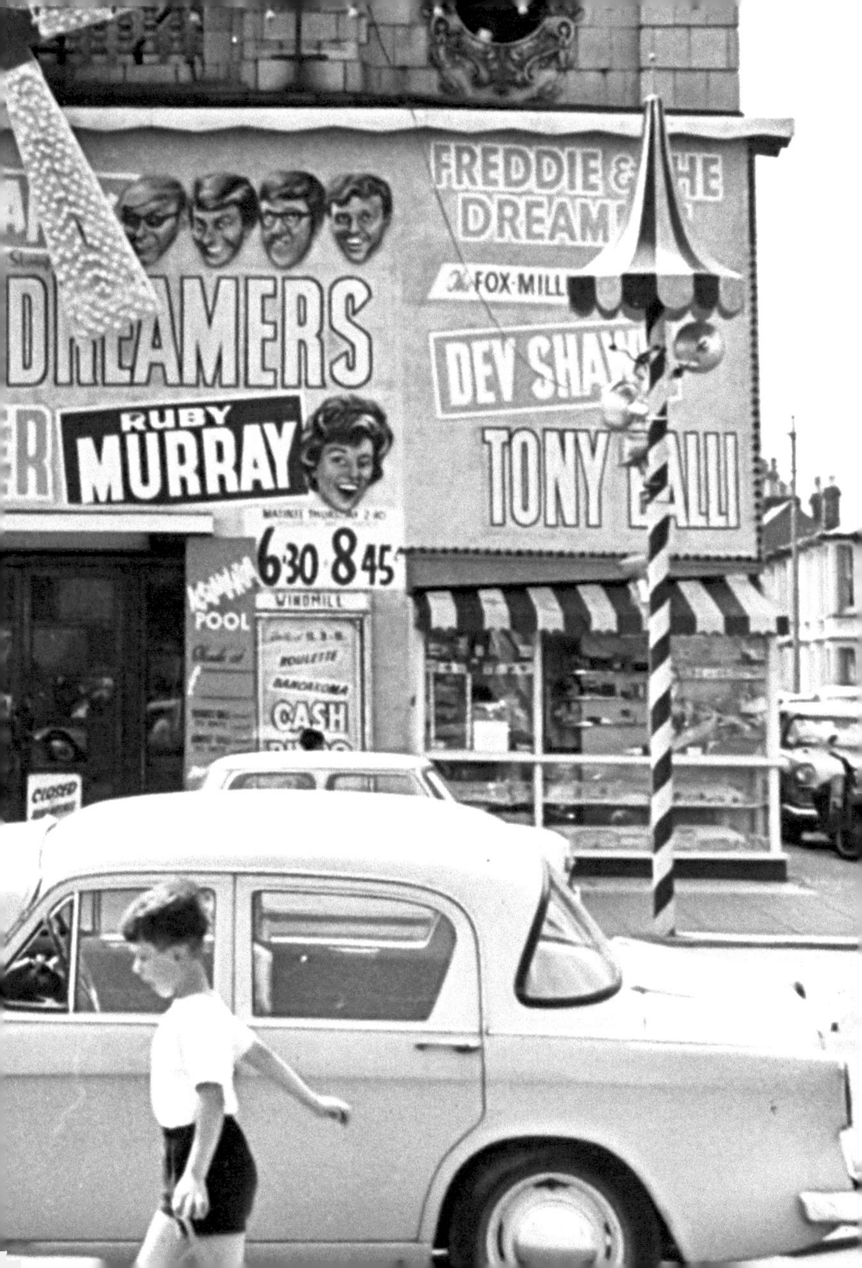
DREAMERS
FREDDIE & THE DREAMERS
FOX·MILL
DEV SHAW
RUBY MURRAY
TONY ALLI
6·30 8·45
POOL
WINDMILL
ROULETTE
CASH
CLOSED

28. AMUSEMENT ARCADES AND THE EMPIRE

The two buildings here capture the essence of past and present Great Yarmouth. The two semi-circular arches in the left-hand building mark the entrances to the Marine Arcades, built in 1902 and 1904 and originally containing twenty shops, all catering for the holiday trade. The Empire Cinema opened in 1911. It was then described as a 'handsome terracotta elevation, the striking features of which are lofty columns and a large semi-circular balcony'.

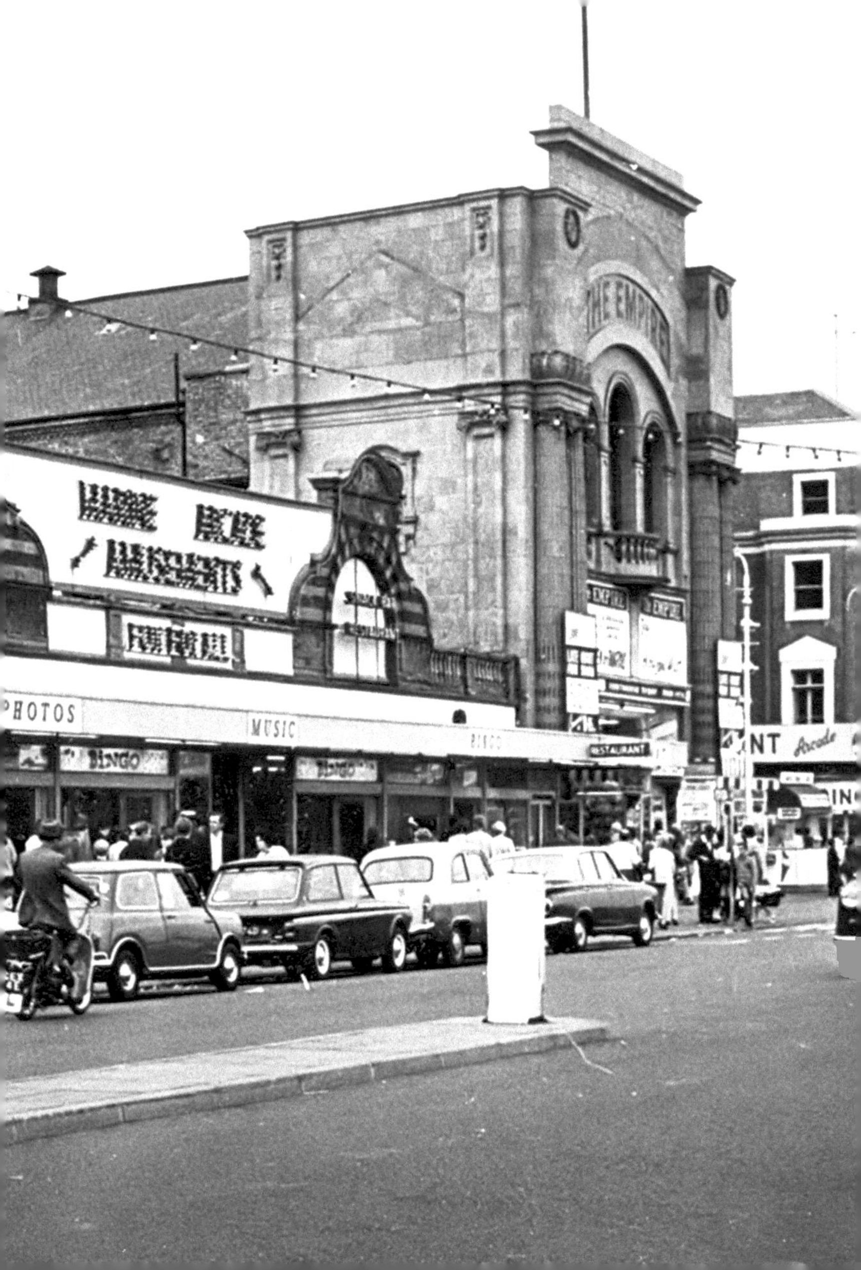

29. TRAMS AND BUSES IN FRONT OF BRITANNIA PIER

The electric tramways in Yarmouth opened in 1902; an earlier horse-drawn tramway had run to Gorleston since 1875. Even in the 1930s, a tram ride from the north end of Yarmouth to the Wellington Pier cost only two pence, and a trip from the top of Regent Road to Wellington Pier cost just one penny!

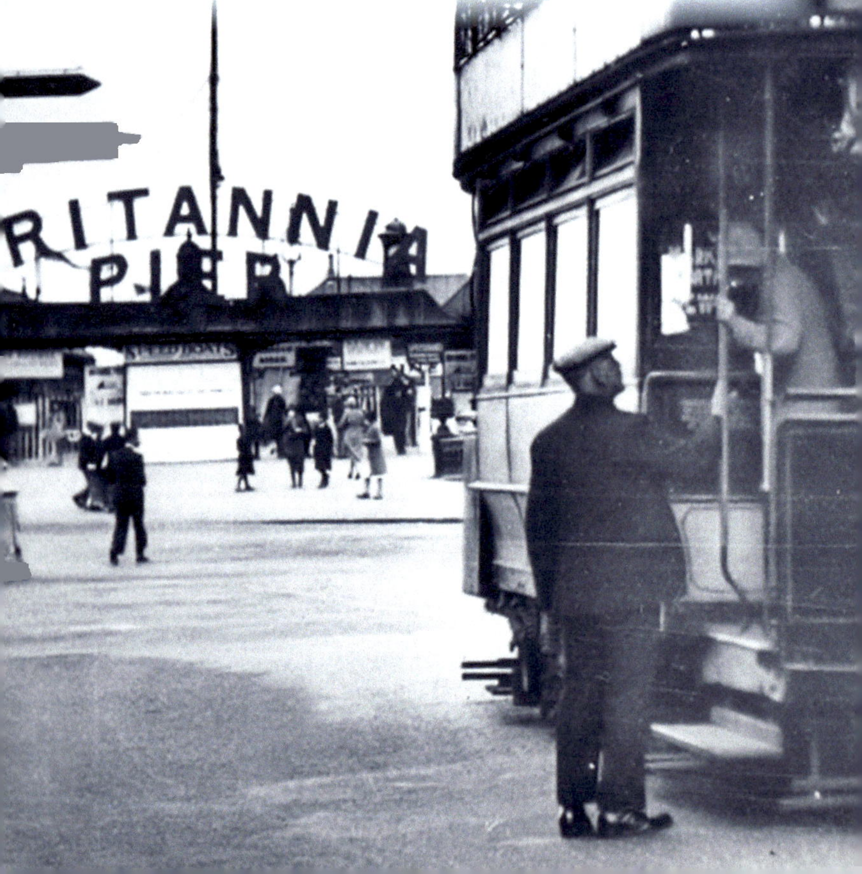

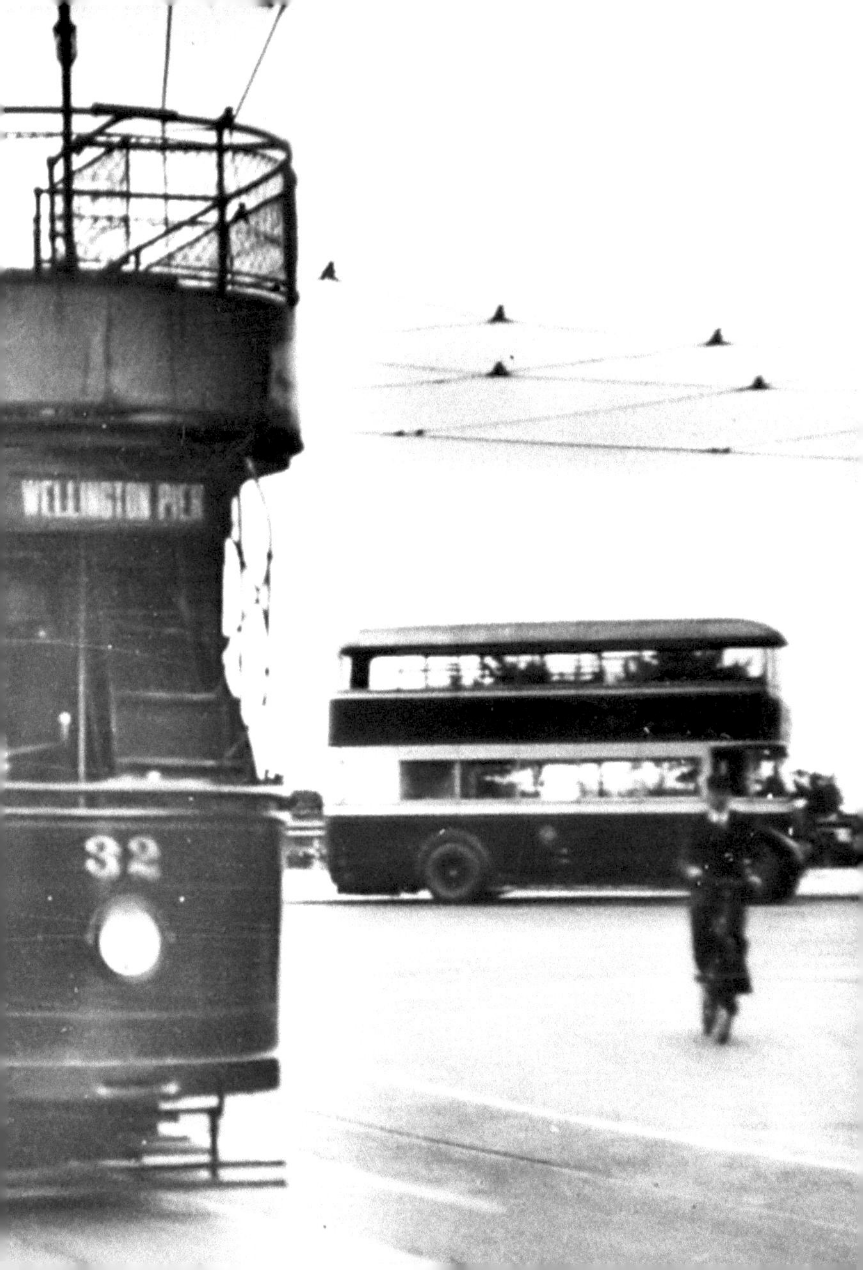

WELLINGTON PIER
32

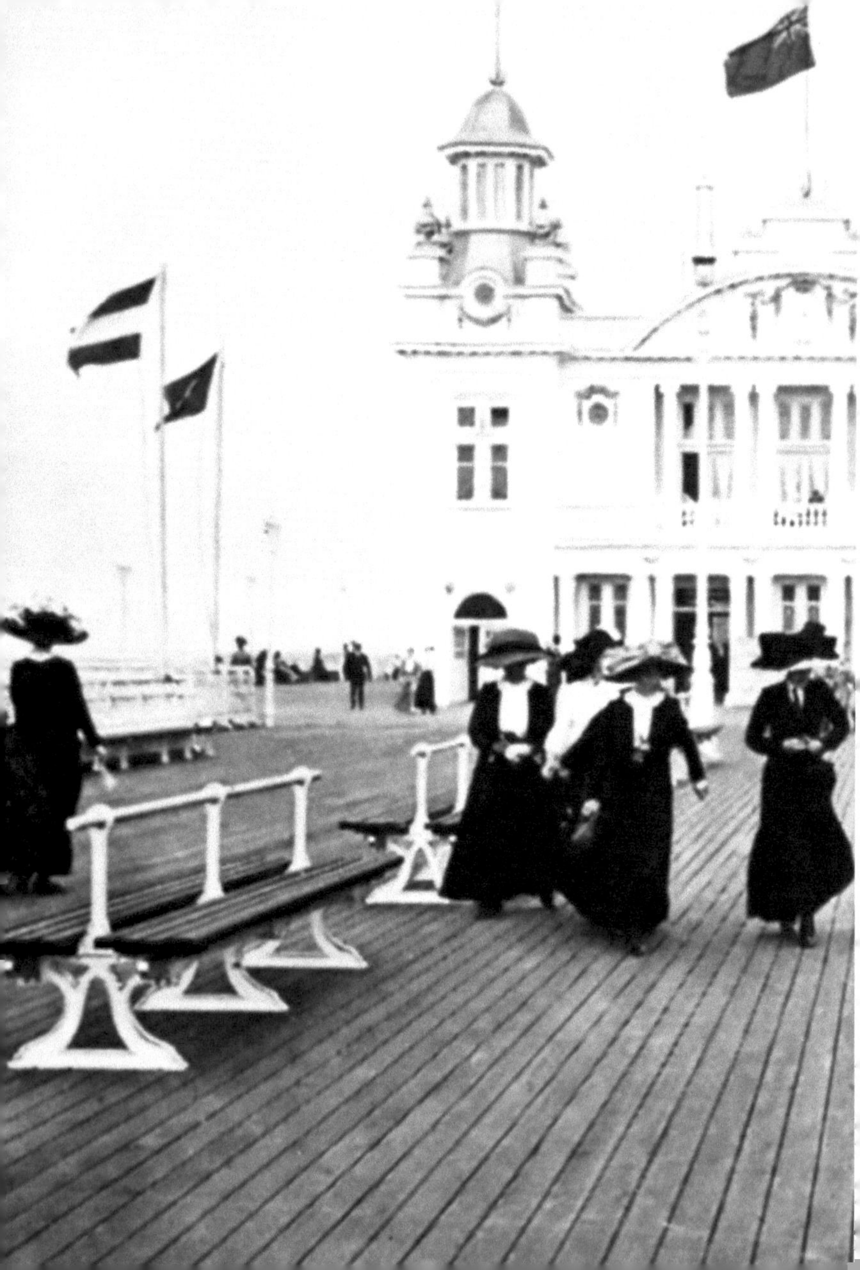

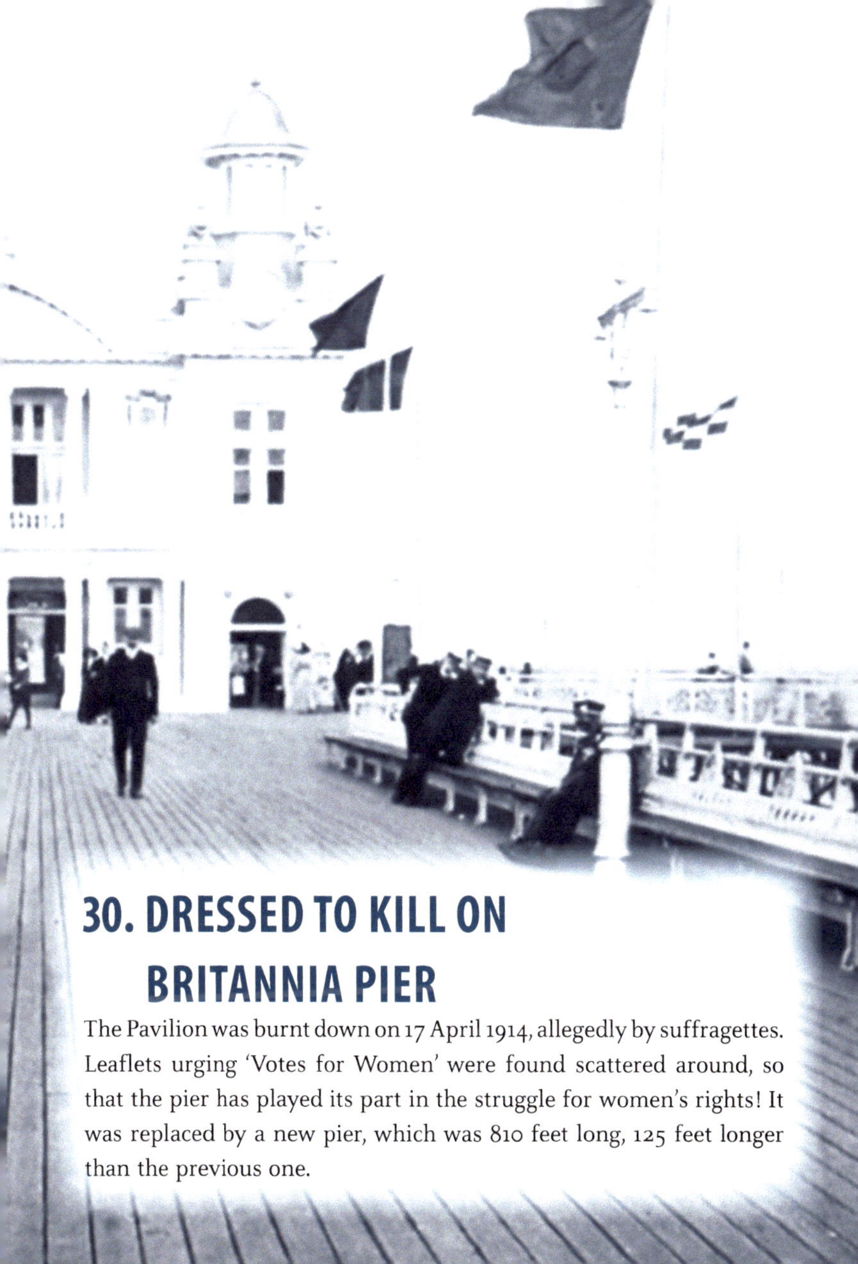

30. DRESSED TO KILL ON BRITANNIA PIER

The Pavilion was burnt down on 17 April 1914, allegedly by suffragettes. Leaflets urging 'Votes for Women' were found scattered around, so that the pier has played its part in the struggle for women's rights! It was replaced by a new pier, which was 810 feet long, 125 feet longer than the previous one.

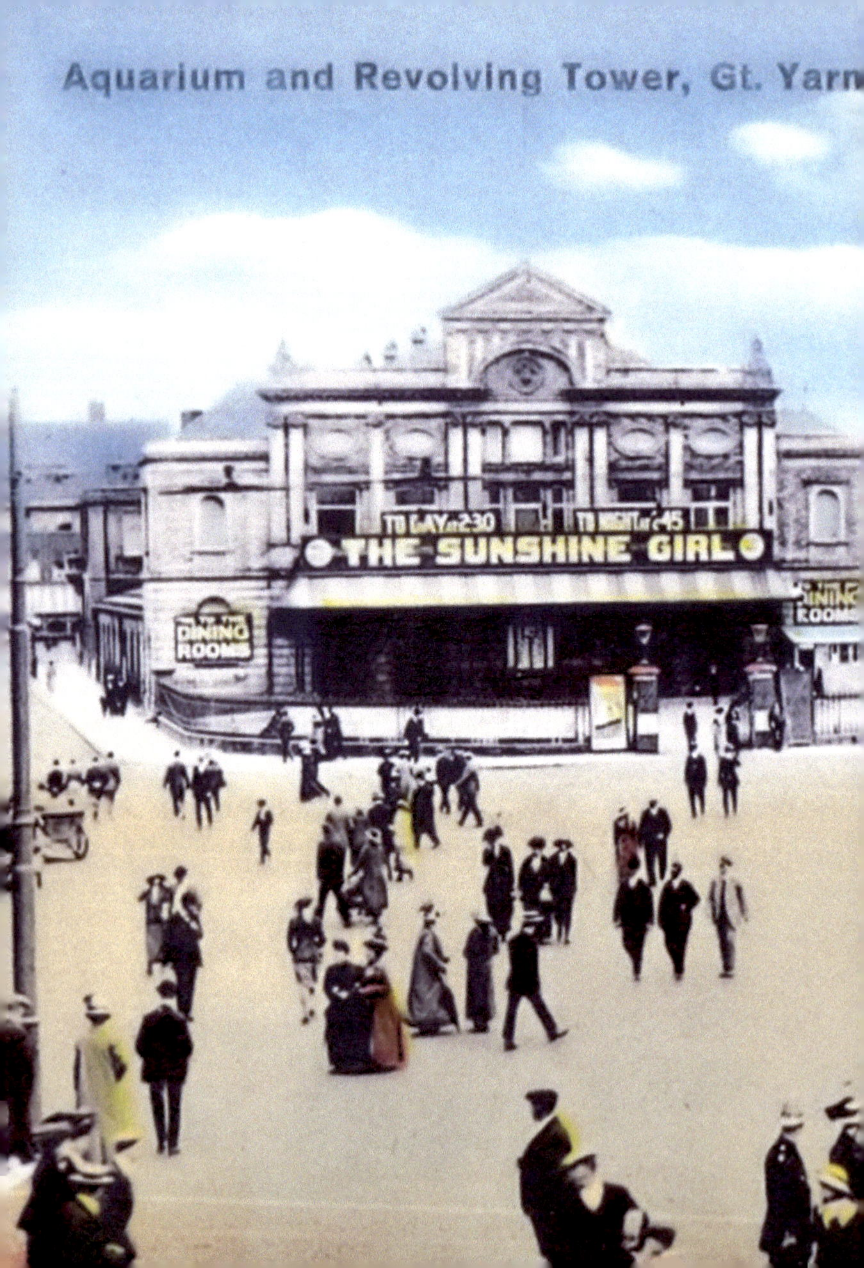

Aquarium and Revolving Tower, Gt. Yarn

TO DAY at 2.30   TO NIGHT at 7.45
THE SUNSHINE GIRL
DINING ROOMS
DINING ROOMS

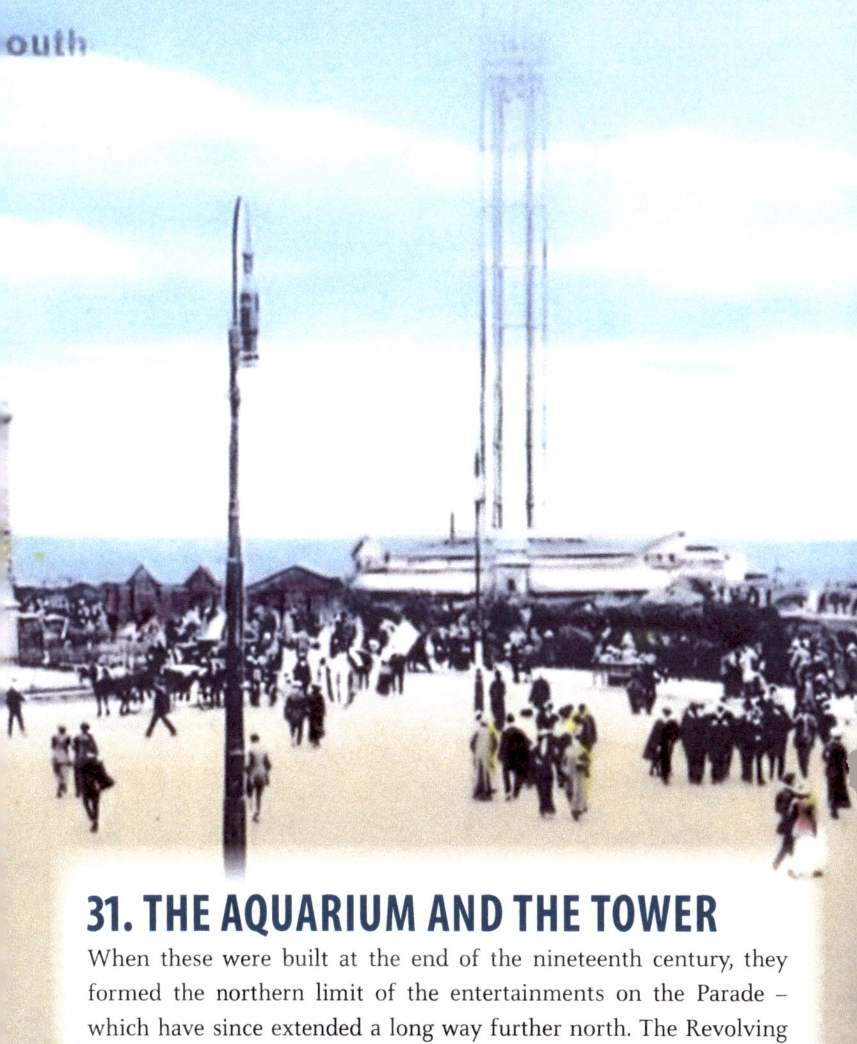

31. THE AQUARIUM AND THE TOWER

When these were built at the end of the nineteenth century, they formed the northern limit of the entertainments on the Parade – which have since extended a long way further north. The Revolving Observation Tower was demolished in 1941 to provide metal to make armaments.

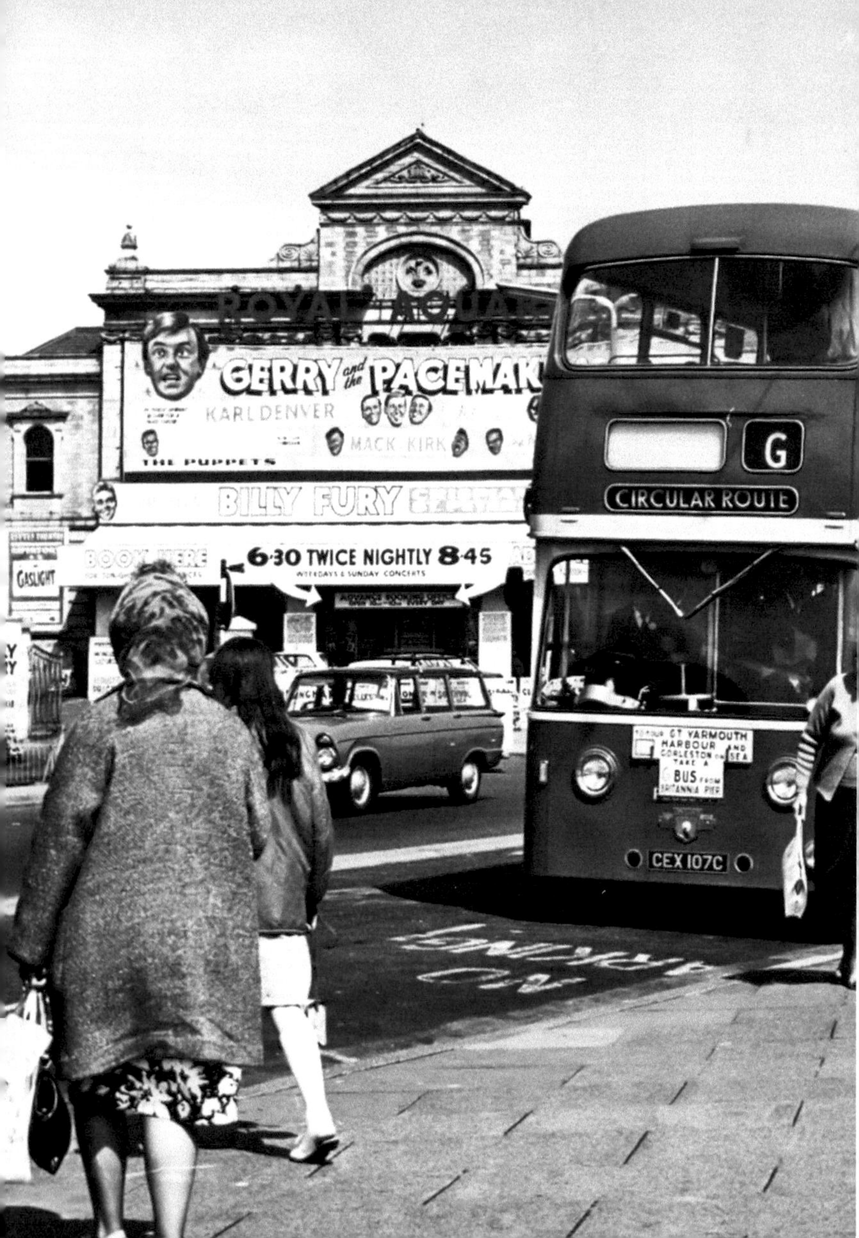

ROYAL AQUAR
GERRY and the PACEMAKERS
KARL DENVER
MACK KIRK
THE PUPPETS
BILLY FURY
GASLIGHT
BOOK HERE
6·30 TWICE NIGHTLY 8·45
WEEKDAYS & SUNDAY CONCERTS
ADVANCE BOOKING OFFICE
OPEN 10AM TO 8PM EVERY DAY
G
CIRCULAR ROUTE
FOR GT YARMOUTH
HARBOUR AND
GORLESTON ON SEA
TAKE A
G BUS FROM
BRITANNIA PIER
CEX 107C

32. THE AQUARIUM: ENTERTAINMENT CENTRE

The aquarium opened in 1883 and became a theatre in 1896, although a few of the fish tanks were retained, an early version of the modern Sea Life. Oscar Wilde once gave a lecture here. It became a cinema in 1914 and also hosted popular musical comedies and, later, live-music groups. It was renamed the Royalty in 1982 and the Hollywood in 1992.

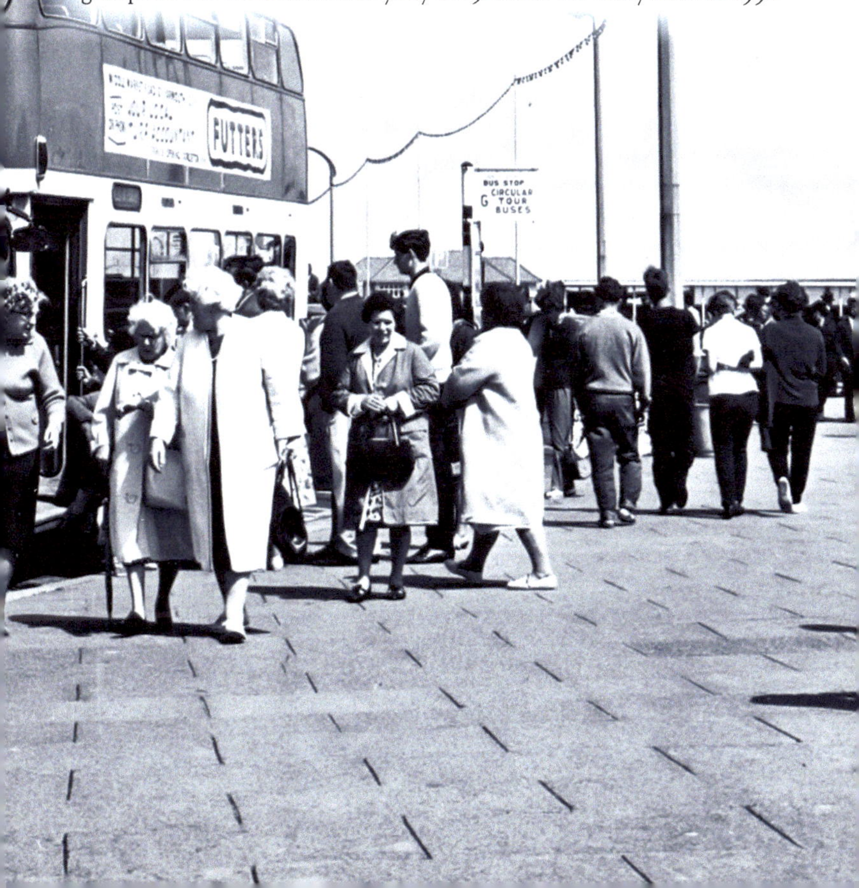

33. THE BOATING LAKE

Something on the lake seems to have caught the attention of most of the people in this image, perhaps the traditional call of 'Come in, number five, your time is up!' The people on the extreme left are on the parade; the beach and the sea are immediately behind the wall on the far side of the lake.

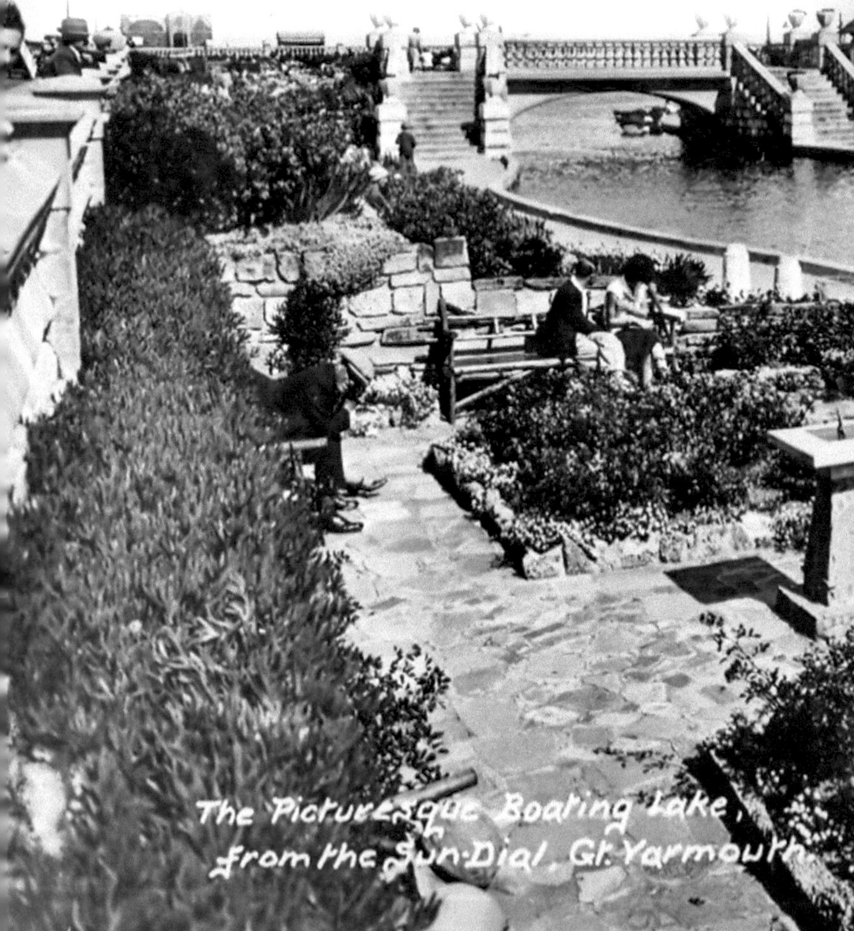

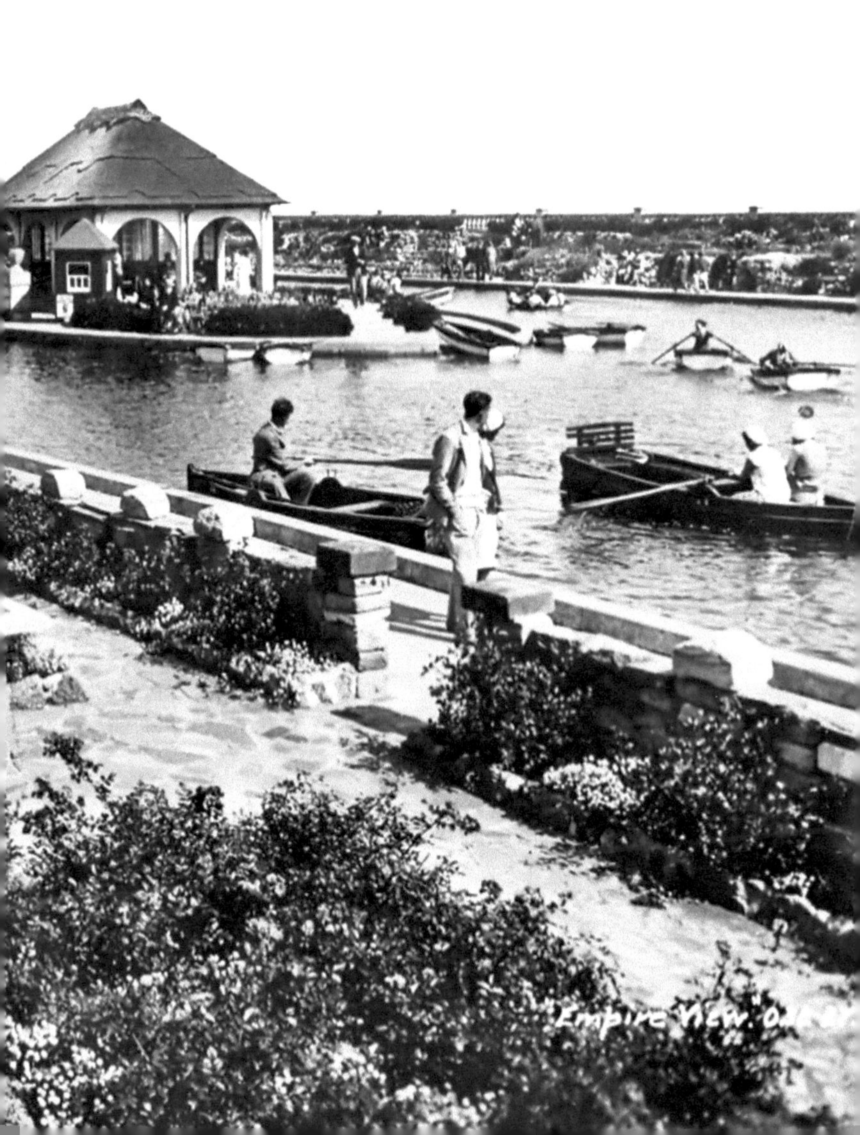

Empire View. Oa

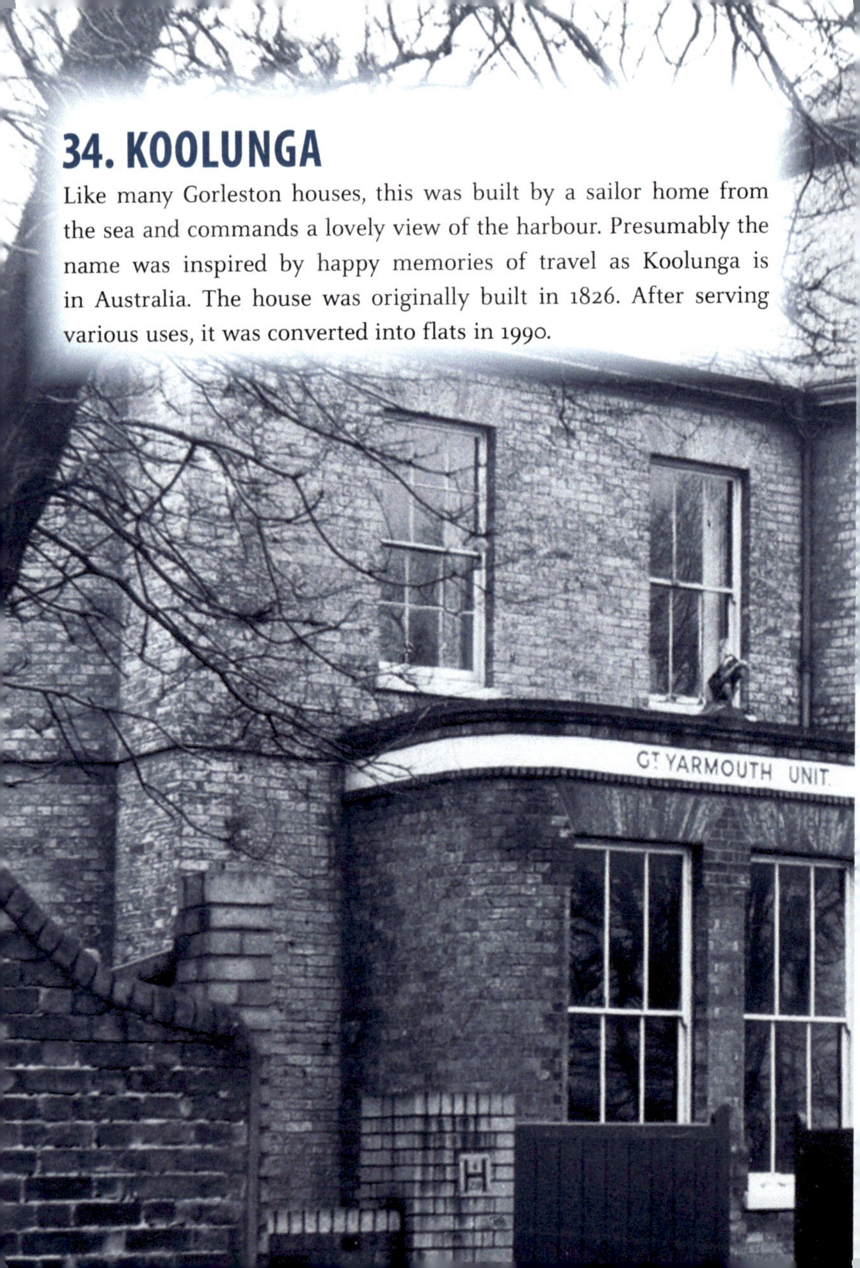

34. KOOLUNGA

Like many Gorleston houses, this was built by a sailor home from the sea and commands a lovely view of the harbour. Presumably the name was inspired by happy memories of travel as Koolunga is in Australia. The house was originally built in 1826. After serving various uses, it was converted into flats in 1990.

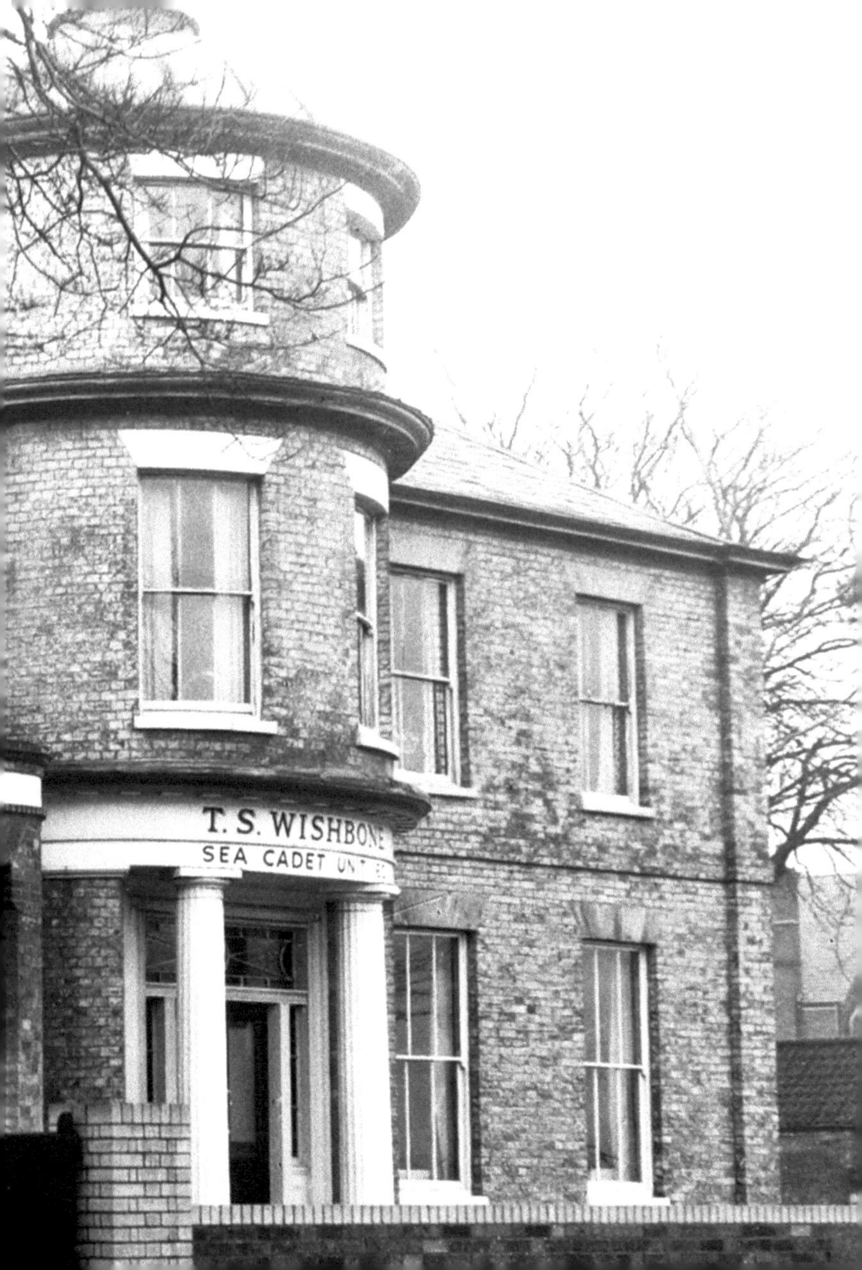
T. S. WISHBONE
SEA CADET UNIT

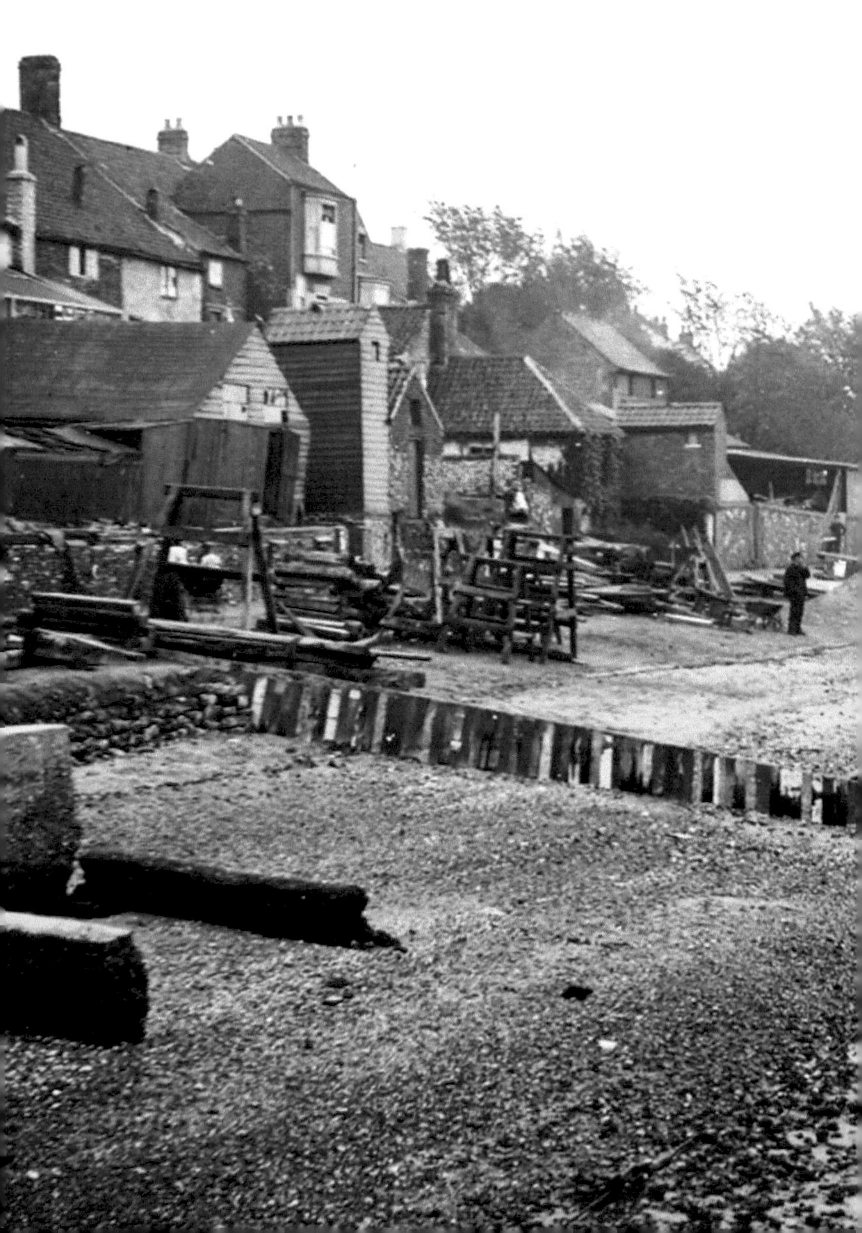

35. SHIPBUILDING

Gorleston was not just a holiday town, it had an important industrial side to it as well and there were many shipbuilding and repairing yards. The activity has completely gone today, but one or two parts of the sea front retain a flavour of their past.

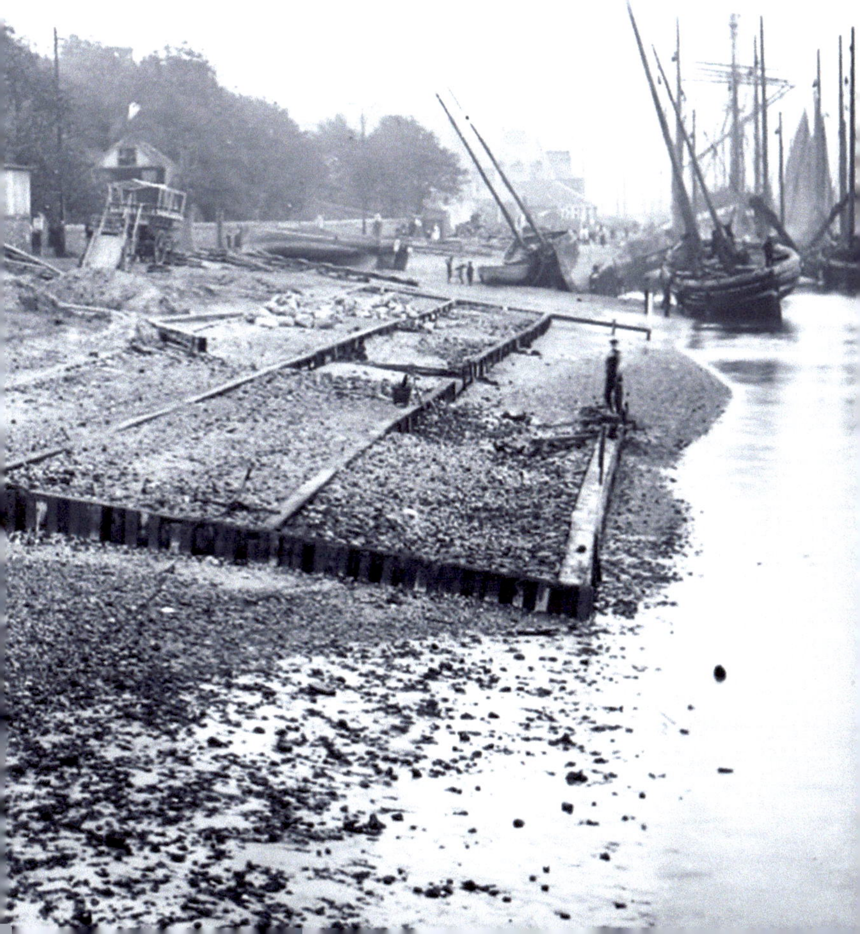

36. A DUTCH GABLE IN GORLESTON

This form of gable is taken from a style used in Holland. There are close links across the North Sea between Yarmouth and the Netherlands, only ninety miles away, and when Germany invaded Belgium and the Netherlands on 10 May 1940 the sound of the guns could be heard like thunder here in Gorleston!

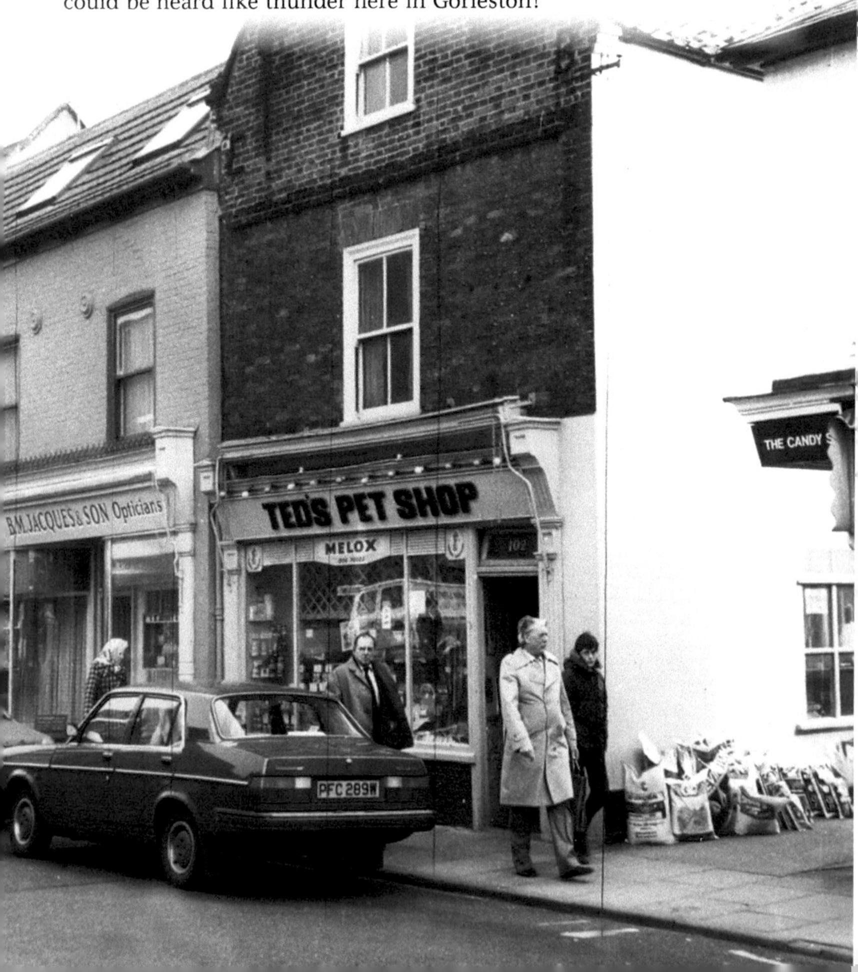

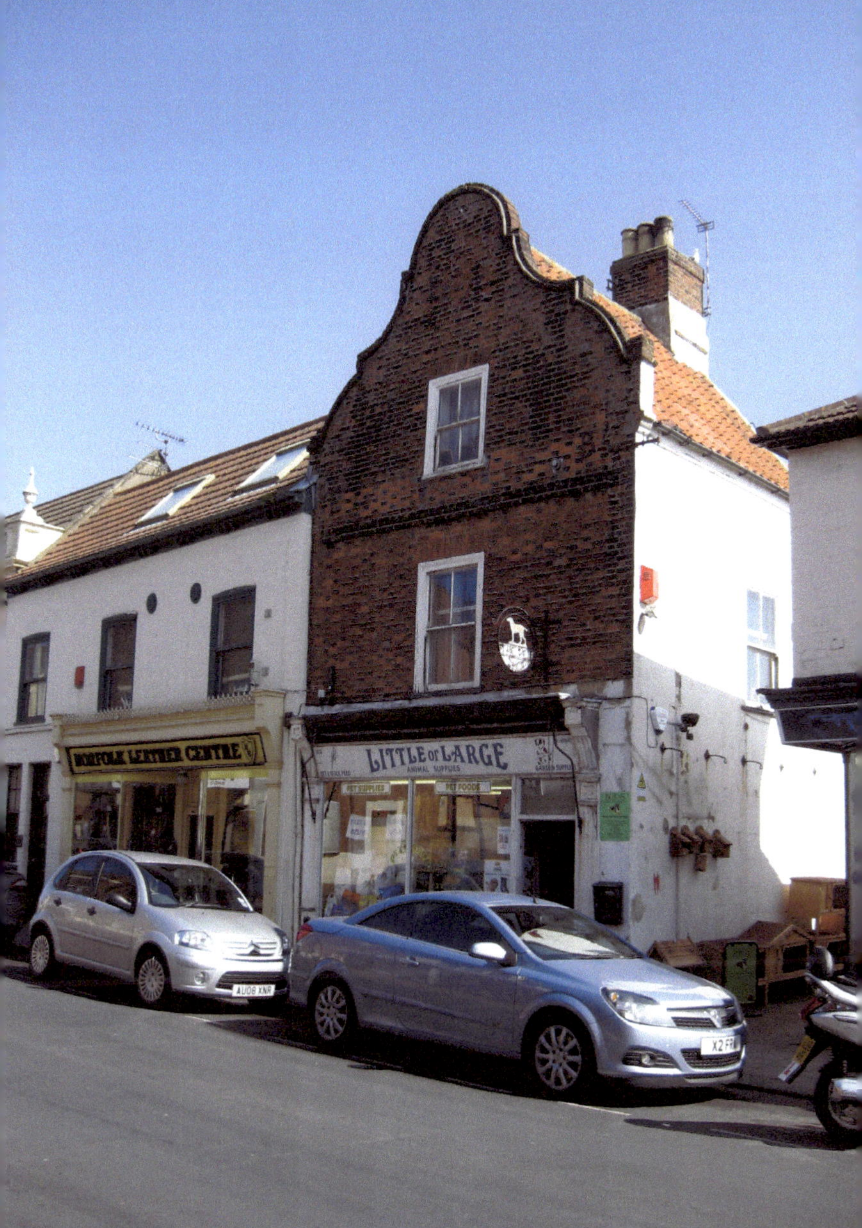

NORFOLK LEATHER CENTRE
LITTLE or LARGE
ANIMAL SUPPLIES
PET SUPPLIES
PET FOODS

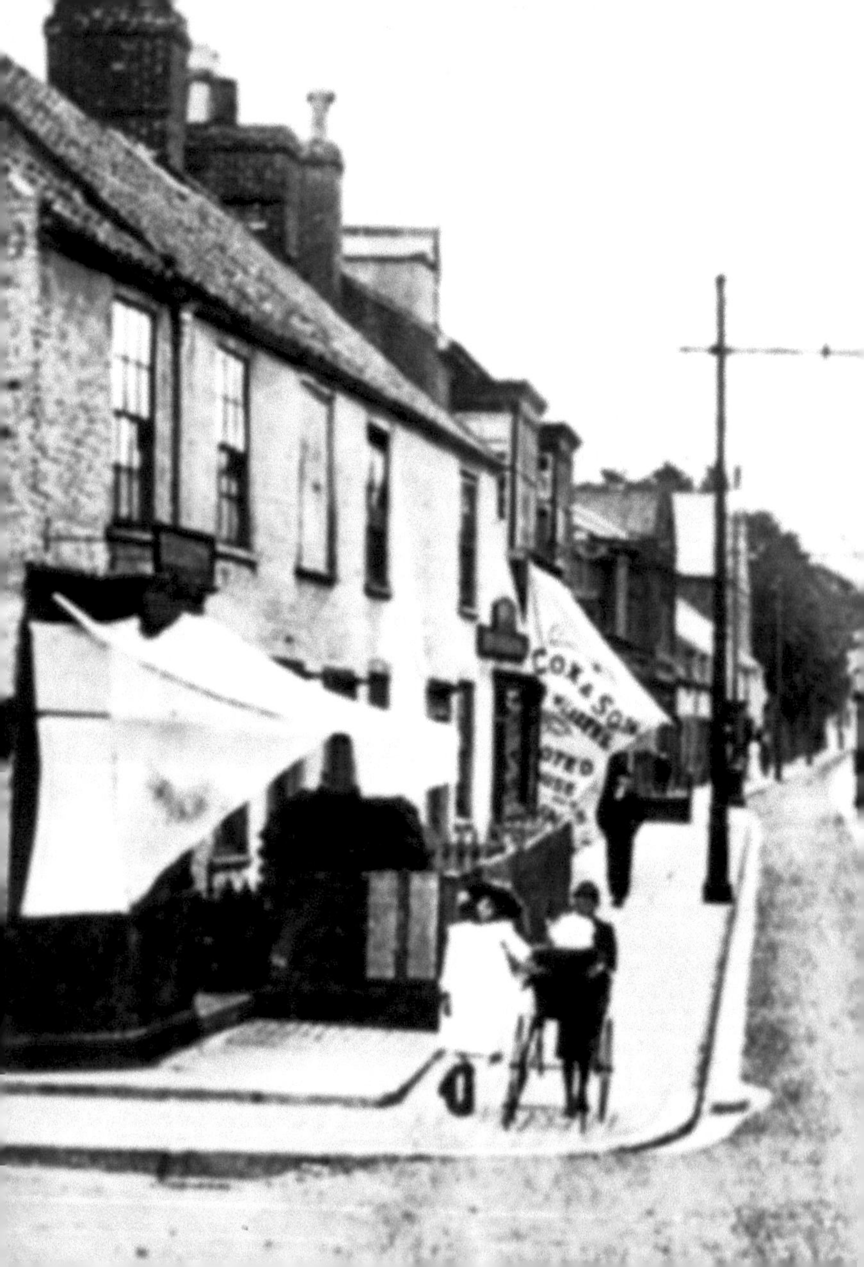
COR & SON

37. HIGH STREET WITH TRAM

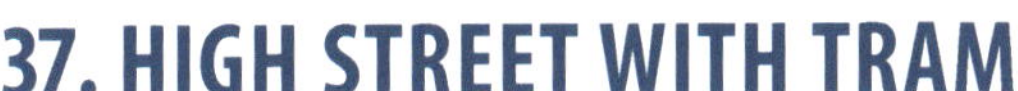

Gorleston was linked by tram with the Haven Bridge in the centre of Yarmouth as early as 1875; for the first twenty-five years the trams were pulled by horses. The line was electrified in 1900. There was never a tramline across the Haven Bridge so passengers had to walk across and board another tram on the other side of the river!

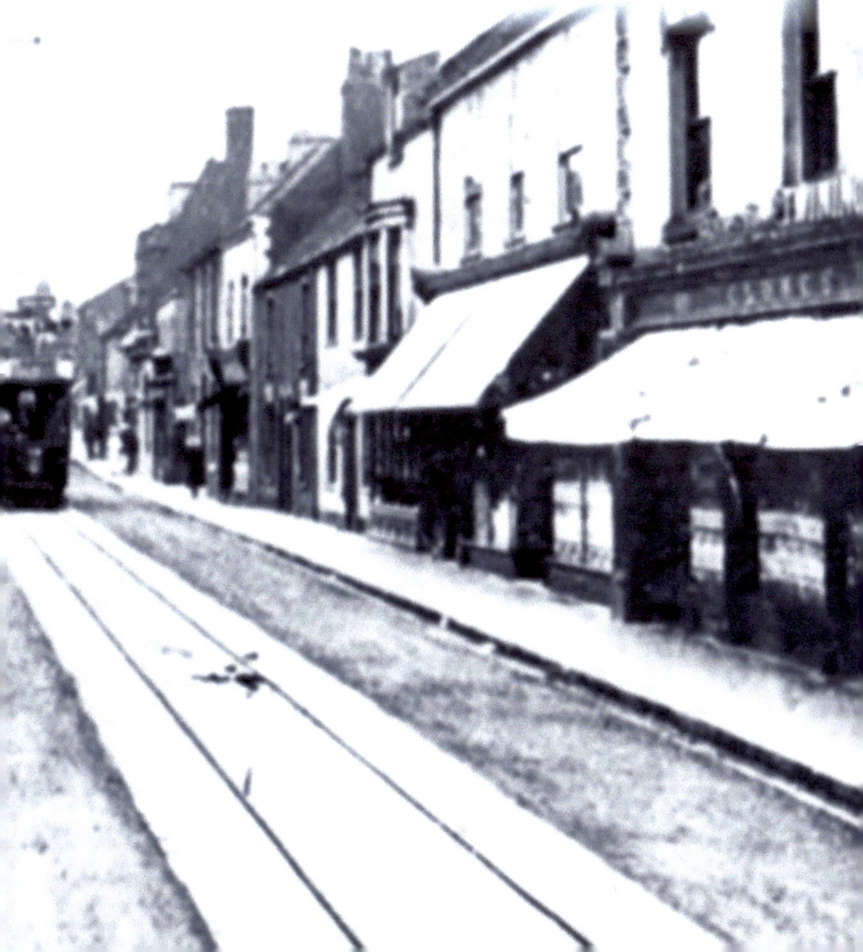

38. GORLESTON TRAM DEPOT

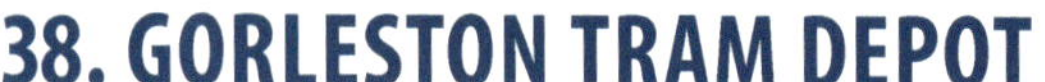

The tram depot, opposite the Feathers, did not last long, being replaced by the Carnegie Library in 1907. This was itself demolished in the 1970s to make way for the new library, which opened in 1977. Only the name and the sign of another public house beyond the library – the Tramway – reminds present-day Gorleston residents of the trams.

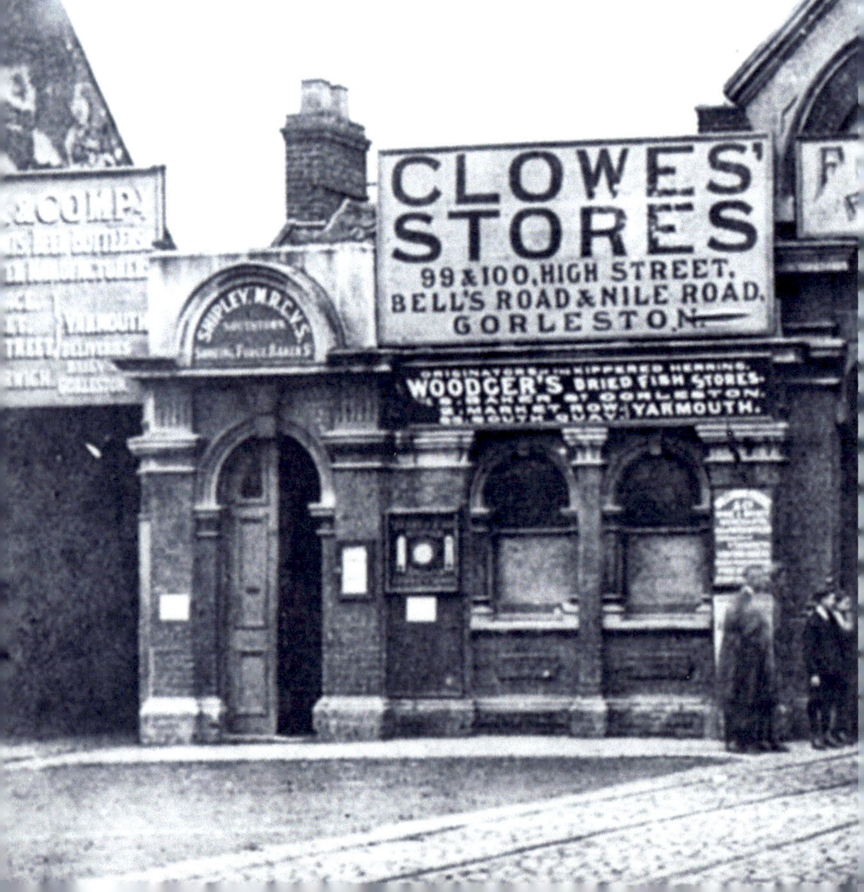

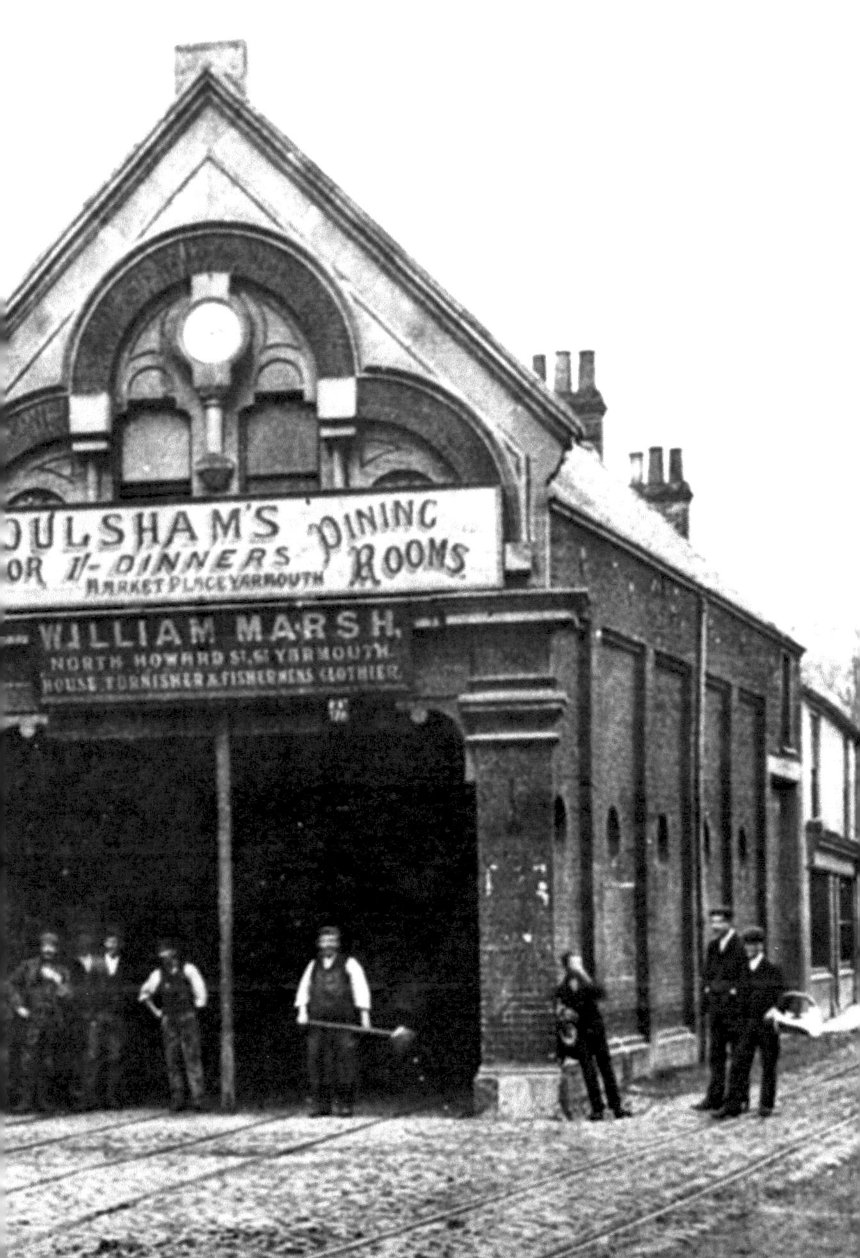
OULSHAM'S
OR 1/- DINNERS
MARKET PLACE YARMOUTH
DINING
ROOMS
WILLIAM MARSH,
NORTH HOWARD ST. GT YARMOUTH
HOUSE FURNISHER & FISHERMENS CLOTHIER.

39. CLIFF HILL

In this photograph we are looking along one of the loveliest streets in Norfolk, running along the side of Gorleston 'cliff' and with beautiful views of the harbour – we could almost be in a Cornish or Devon fishing village. Beachmen and pilots were the first to build houses here from the early nineteenth century. There is a distant view of the Nelson monument in Yarmouth from this street.

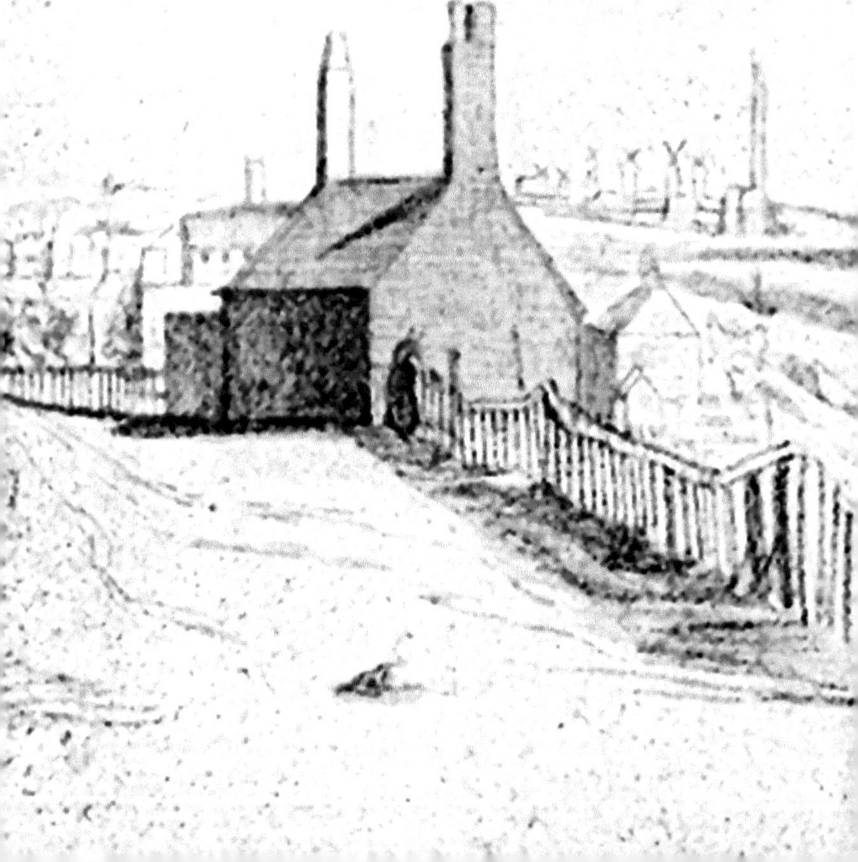

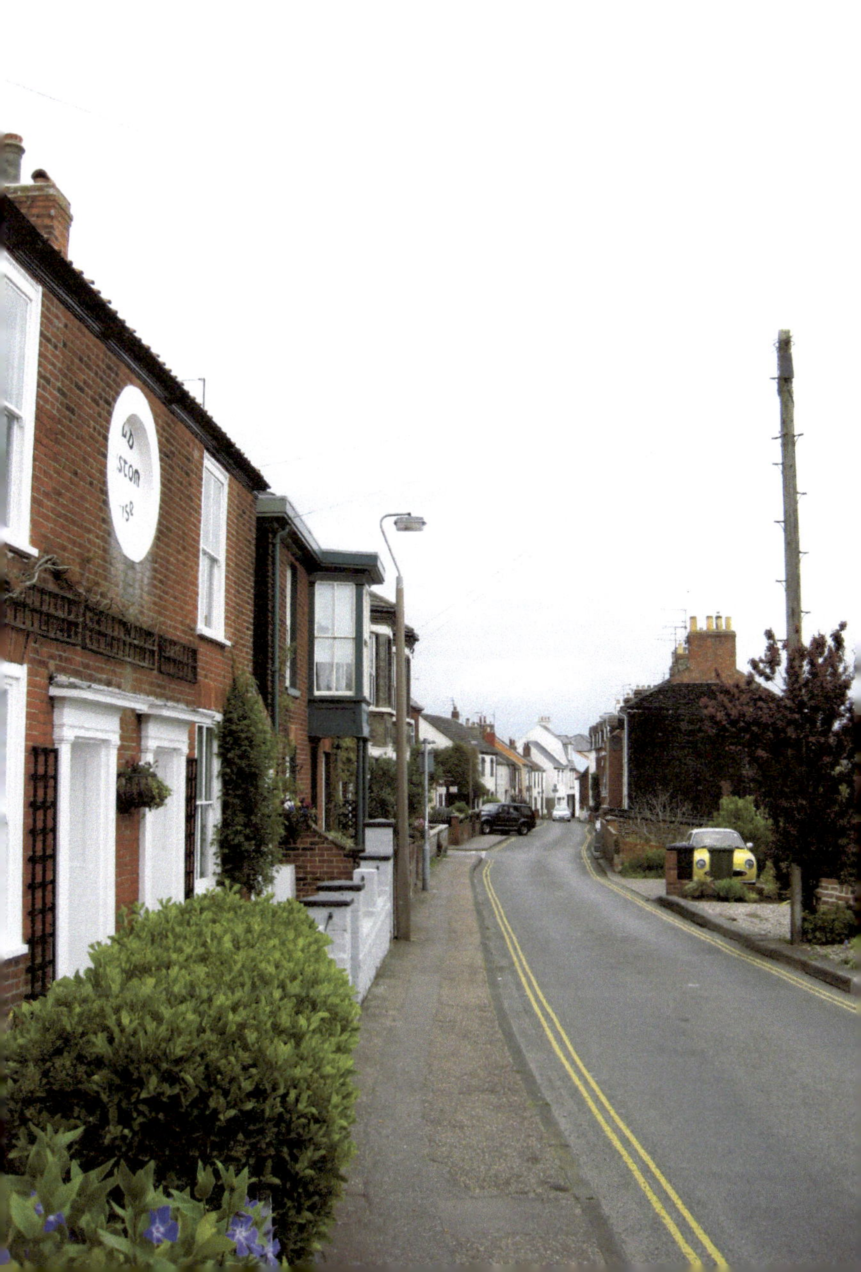
OLD
CUSTOM
HOUSE

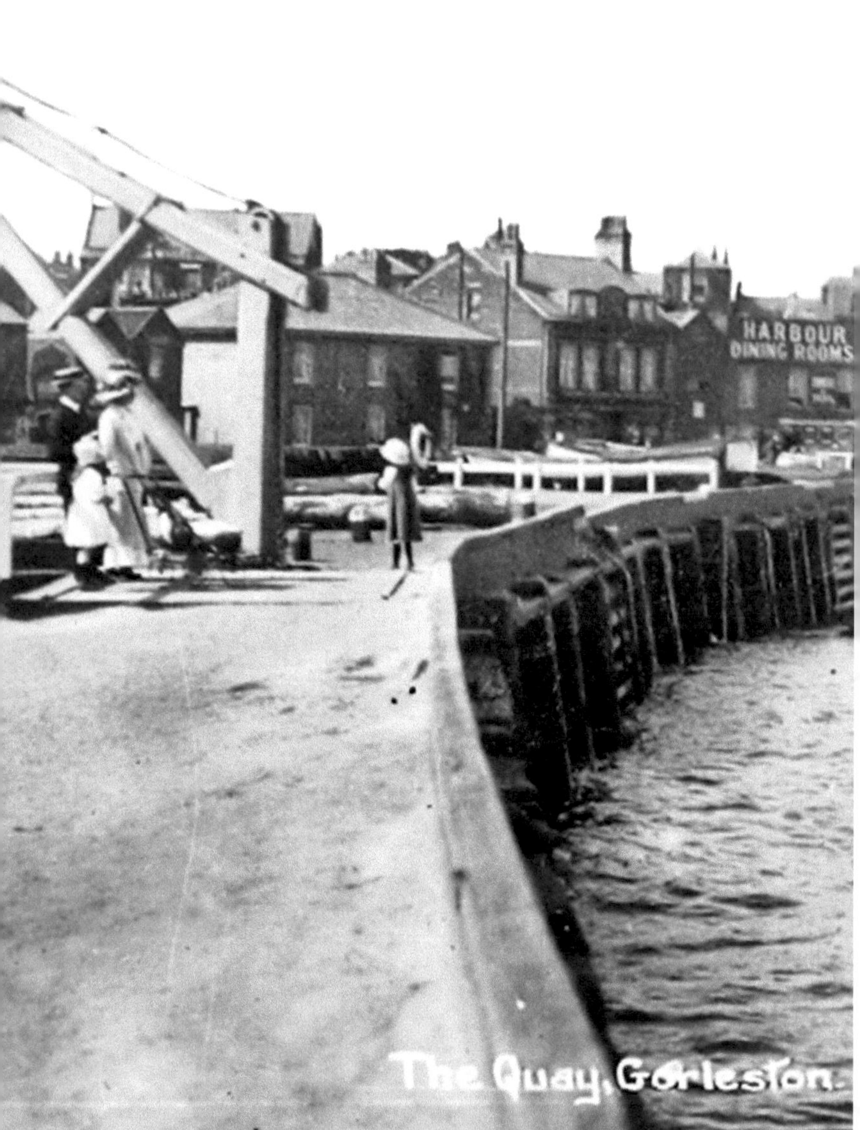

HARBOUR
DINING ROOMS
The Quay, Gorleston

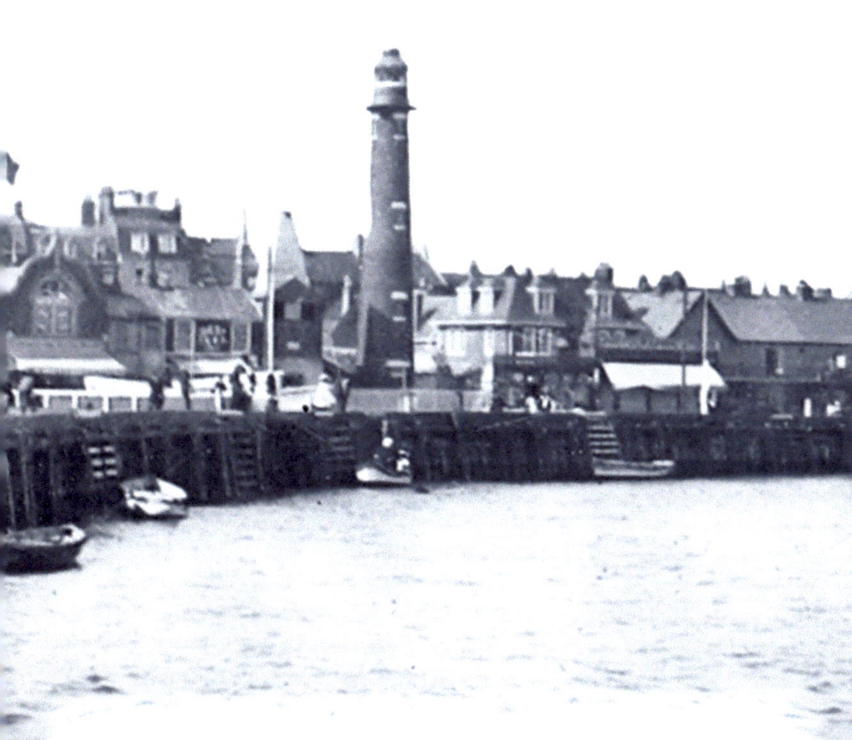

40. THE QUAY

Gorleston Lighthouse was built by Great Yarmouth Port and Haven Commissioners in 1887 to direct ships into the mouth of the harbour. The dramatic curve in the river can be seen well in these two images. Older residents still recall the unique scent of the area, the fragrant odour of pitch-pine which was unloaded along the river.

41. THE HARBOUR

It is still possible, as it was a century ago, to hear 'the sound of the deep sea booming beyond the two piers that protect with their sheltering arms the harbour mouth at Gorleston'. There have been many attempts to fix the mouth of the river Yare over the centuries. The present outlet was designed by a Dutch engineer, Joos Johnson, who strengthened the sharp bend in the river by hedging it with stakes, piles and brushwood, giving it its present name of Brush Quay.

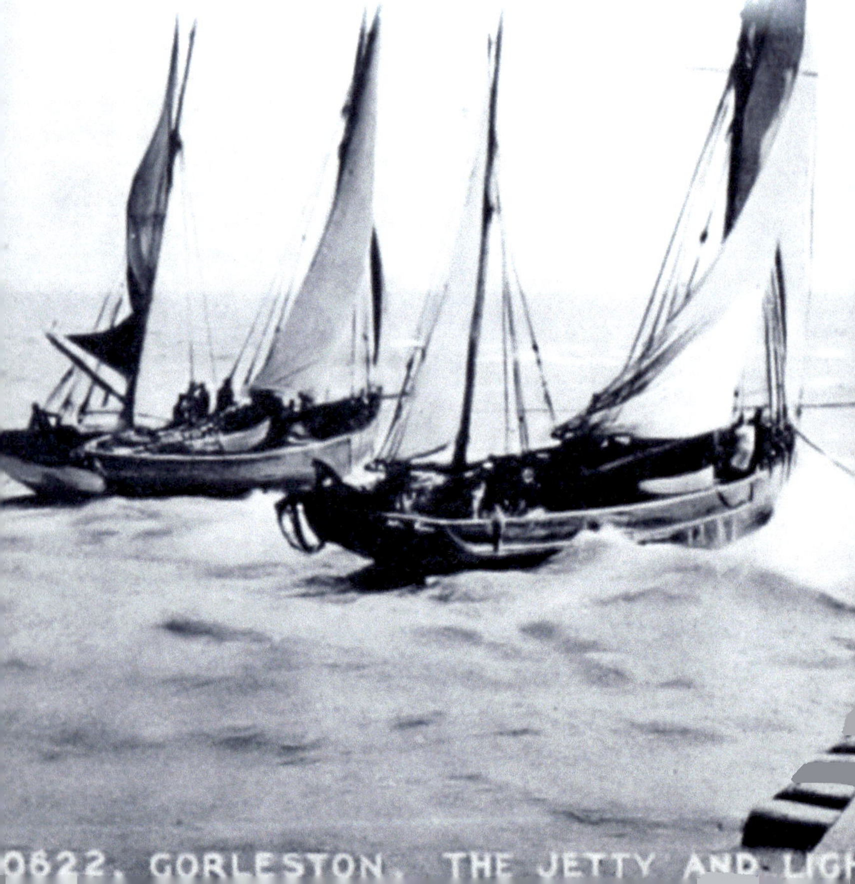

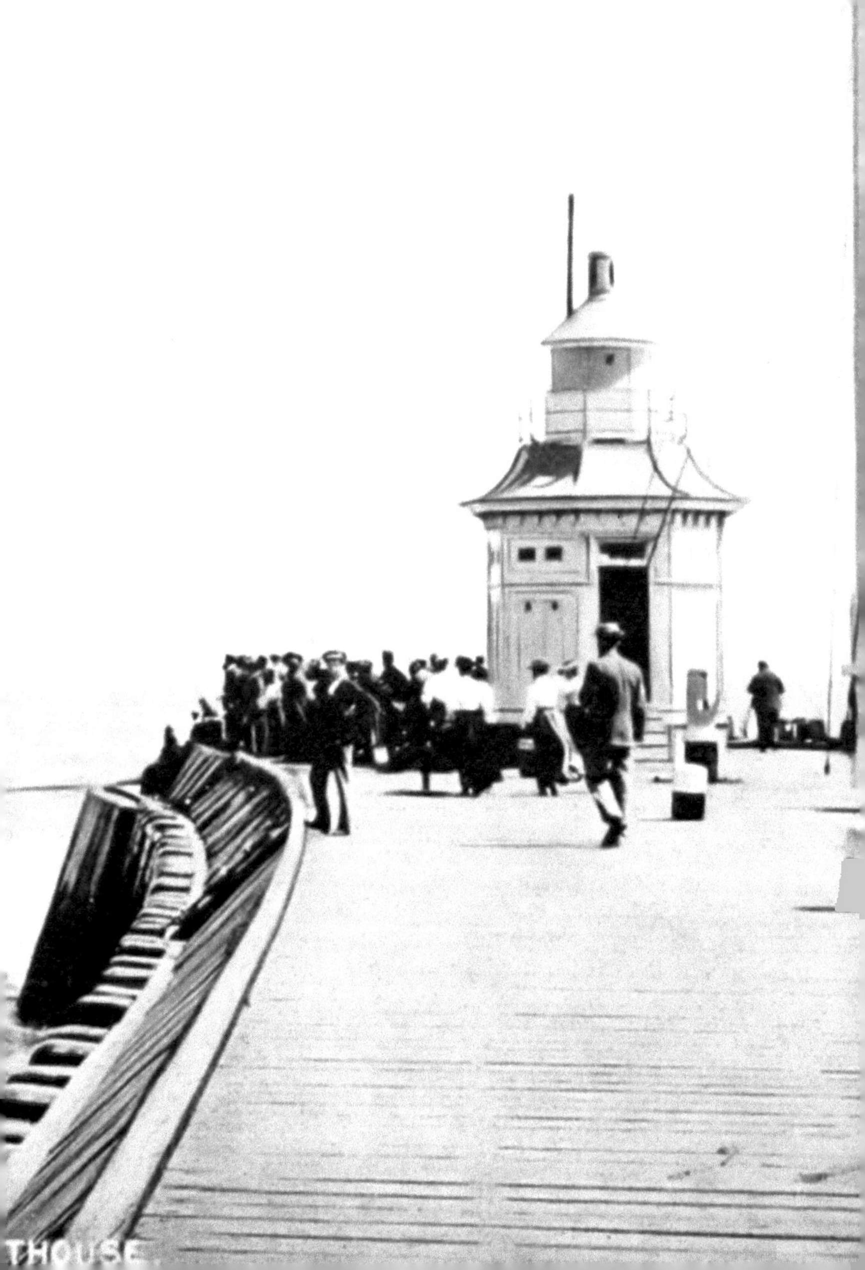

THOUSE

42. THE BEACH AND THE HOTEL

The grand Cliff Hotel opened in 1898. It was designed by the Norwich architect George Skipper. From 1910, a guide reads, 'It is difficult to realize that on the spot where the Cliff Hotel now stands, a rustic windmill waved gaunt arms a few years ago over an expanse of wild heath'. The life of the hotel was a short one, however, as it was destroyed by fire on Boxing Day 1915.

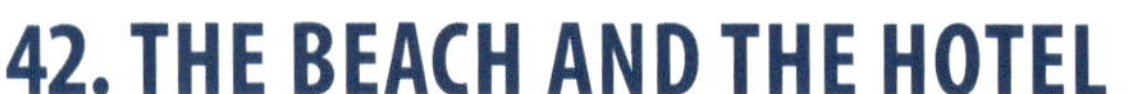

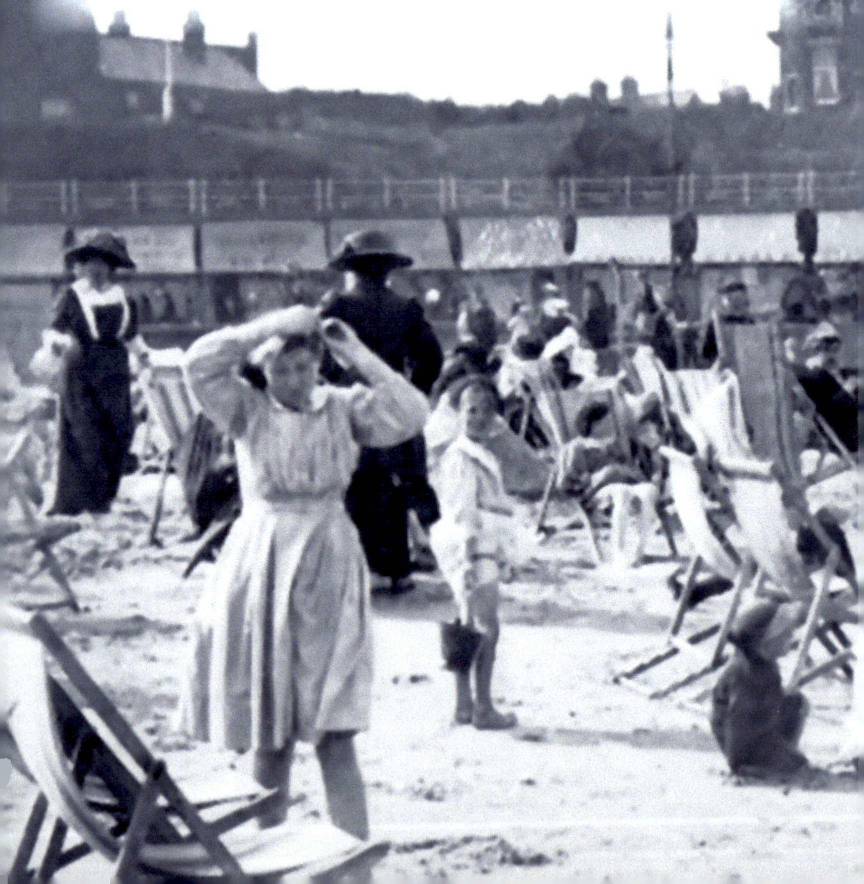

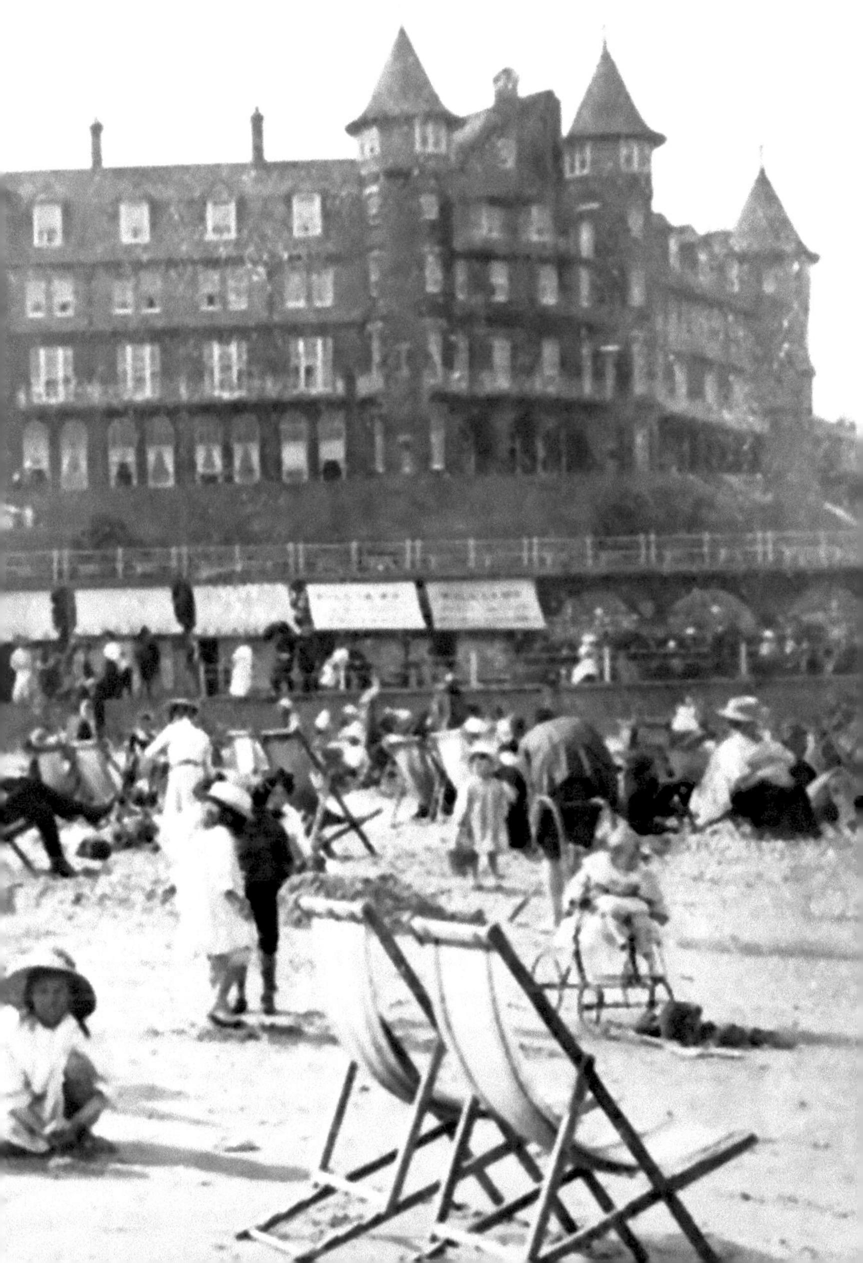

43. THE MODEL YACHT POND

The Yacht Pond was built in 1926, as part of a series of schemes by the Borough Council to supply work to the unemployed. It makes a happy souvenir from a distressing time of mass unemployment and poverty, and is still well used by local enthusiasts.

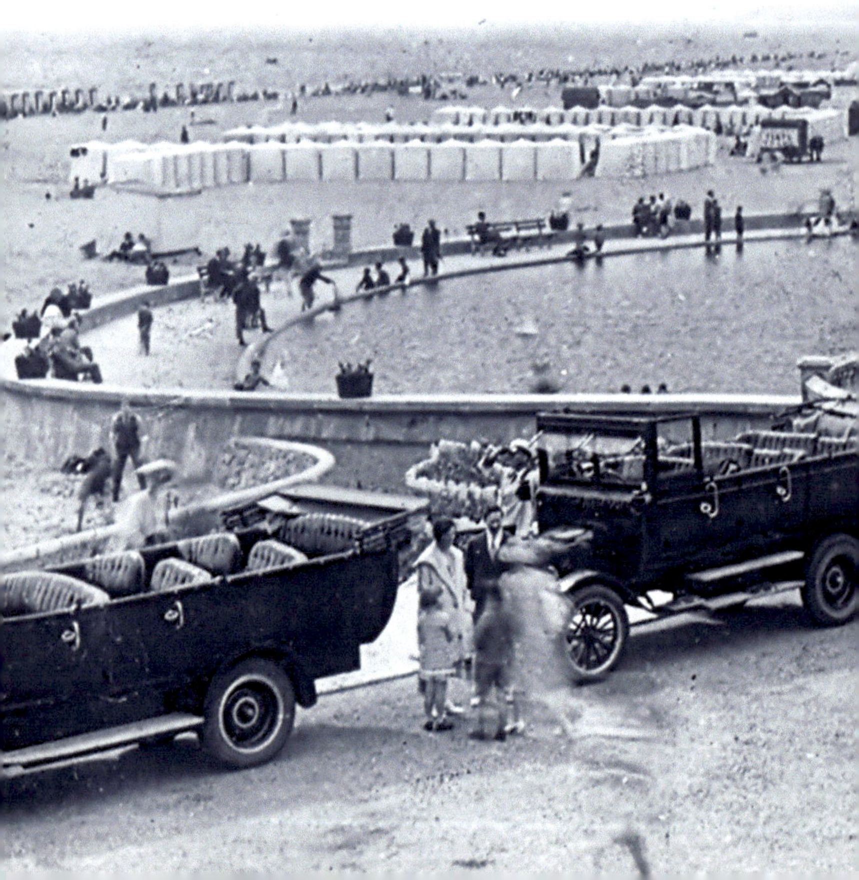

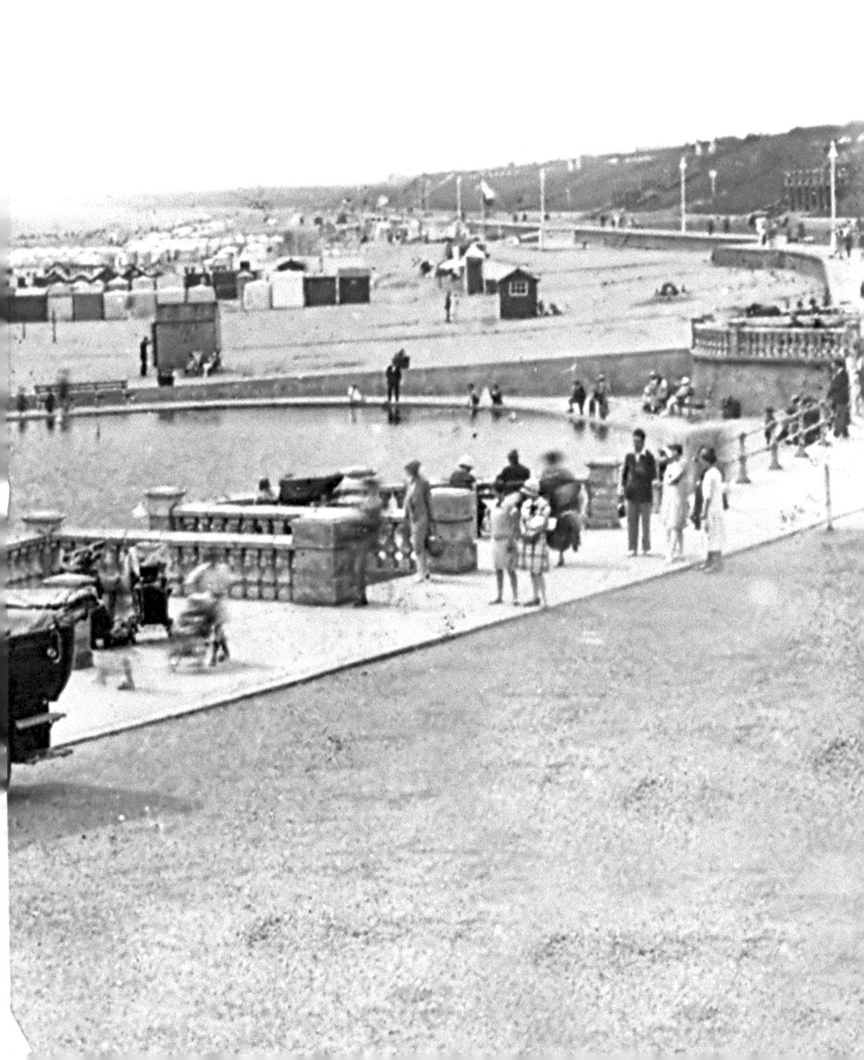

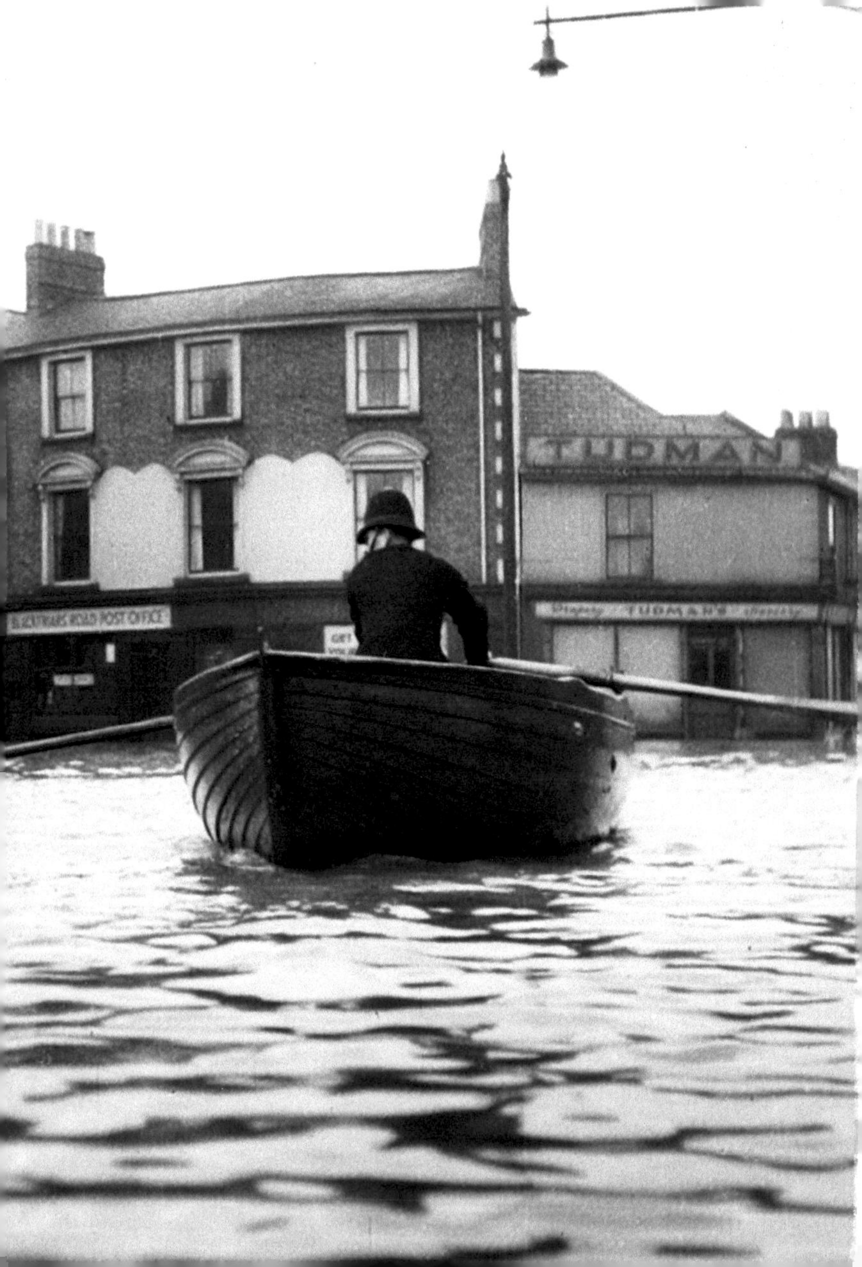

ST. SAVIOURS ROAD POST OFFICE
TUDMAN